Afterschool
MATTERS

This book is dedicated to the youth development practitioners who work in out-of-school time programs. They are the ones who often make a lasting impression in the lives of youth and inspire joy, love of learning, and a sense of belonging. I salute and honor their work.

Afterschool
MATTERS

**Creative Programs That Connect
Youth Development and
Student Achievement**

Edited by **Sara Hill**

Foreword by Glynda A. Hull

CORWIN PRESS
A SAGE Publications Company
Thousand Oaks, CA 91320

For information:

Corwin Press
A Sage Publications Company
2455 Teller Road
Thousand Oaks, California 91320
www.corwinpress.com

Sage Publications India Pvt. Ltd.
B 1/I 1 Mohan Cooperative Industrial Area
Mathura Road, New Delhi 110 044
India

Sage Publications Ltd.
1 Oliver's Yard
55 City Road
London EC1Y 1SP
United Kingdom

Sage Publications Asia-Pacific Pte. Ltd.
33 Pekin Street #02-01
Far East Square
Singapore 048763

Printed in the United States of America

Library of Congress Cataloging-in-Publication Data

Afterschool matters: Creative programs that connect youth development and student achievement/Sara Hill, editor.
     p. cm.
Includes bibliographical references and index.
ISBN 978-1-4129-4123-5 (cloth)
ISBN 978-1-4129-4124-2 (pbk.)
    1. After-school programs—United States. 2. Youth development—United States.
3. Student activities—United States. I. Hill, Sara Louisa. II. Title.

LC34.4.A36 2008
371.8'9—dc22   2007011194

This book is printed on acid-free paper.

07 08 09 10 11 12 10 9 8 7 6 5 4 3 2 1

Acquisitions Editor:	Elizabeth Brenkus
Editorial Assistants:	Desirée Enayati, Ena Rosen
Copy Editor:	Karen Taylor
Typesetter:	C&M Digitals (P) Ltd.
Indexer:	Molly Hall
Cover Designer:	Monique Hahn
Graphic Designer:	Lisa Riley

Contents

Foreword

Afterschool Talks Back[1]

Glynda A. Hull
University of California, Berkeley

In a recent report Kirsch, Braun, Yamamoto, and Sum (2007) warn America of the gathering of a "perfect storm," the confluence of three forces that they believe threatens the country's economic well-being and its social compact. As the authors point out, each of these three forces alone is something to be reckoned with; but it's the circumstance of their intermingling that should make us all tremble. First, the distribution of skill among both children and adults has been and remains widely disparate, breaking down along class and ethnic or racial lines. To give but one of the now familiar examples, graduation rates in the United States have fallen from their peak of 77 percent in 1969 to 70 percent in 1995, where they have remained the same or even significantly worsened for persons of color. At the same time, vast shifts in the U.S. and global economies have radically changed work places, job prospects, and skill requirements. While manufacturing jobs have shrunk to a mere 10 percent of the total employment in the United States, what has increased is the economic benefit of more skills and more education, with lifetime earnings being substantially higher for college graduates. The third force that promises to intersect with disparities in skills and our shifting economy is demographic change. Looking toward the next decades of this century, we will steadily grow older as a population as well as infinitely more diverse. Since many immigrants may not yet possess high school diplomas, employers fear that, as current workers retire, there won't be suitably qualified individuals to take their

---

[1] Many thanks to Mike Rose, Mark Nelson, and Charles Underwood, whose conversations helped me to shape this foreword, and to the staff of the DUSTY afterschool programs in Oakland, CA, whose continual good work continues to inspire.

places. Of greatest concern to readers of this book, however, is the likely consequence that a remotely fair chance at anything approaching the American dream will be less and less available to tens of millions of our students and fellow citizens. Kirsch and colleagues couldn't be starker in their predictions. They believe that we are at a crossroads as a nation—we can choose now, they write, to let people in the United States continue to grow apart, or alternately, "we will invest in efforts to help us grow together" (p. 26).

Admittedly, this is a sober beginning for a foreword to a hopeful book, and perhaps it seems a remote one too, its predictions of near-future economic downturns, even disasters, a far cry from a group of fifth graders testing water samples in an afterschool science project on Manhattan's Lower East Side (Fancsali, this volume) or from African American girls in Nashville "doing hair," all the while happily writing, reading, and talking together during out-of-school time (Edwards, this volume). Yet, I suggest that such economic, demographic, and psychometric trend lines are intertwined, and tightly so, with current pressures that daily play themselves out in schools and afterschool programs, including the lovely portraits offered in this edited volume. Conversely, and even more important, today's afterschool movement, especially as exemplified by such programs as we see described in this book, itself has an important message to send back, a voice to add to the current conversation on how to improve the social futures of our children and our nation. Indeed, I would argue that the afterschool movement should "talk back" in bell hooks's 1989 helpful sense of providing critical and, at times, resistant commentary, "daring to disagree" (p. 5), to disturb the universe by articulating those insights about learning that have been gleaned from a coalescing set of theories, literatures, and practices. These include those associated with youth development (see Hill's introduction to this volume), the New Literacy Studies (Gee, 1996; cf. Hull & Schultz, 2002; Street, 1995), and sociocultural perspectives on learning (cf. Rogoff, 2003). Such a proactive stance of talking back is all the more important at the current moment, when, as Kirsch and colleagues persuasively detail, we sense the gathering of a perfect storm.

Halpern (2004) notes that the nature of out-of-school programs in the United States has varied historically, depending in large part on how the greater society has defined the challenges facing children and youth. At the turn of the century, motivations chiefly included the frank desire to Americanize, to improve habits and morals, especially those of recent immigrants and the poor. The ideologies underpinning some of these Progressive Era programs can make one cringe, so flagrantly jingoistic and ethnocentric do they sound to many twenty-first century ears. In the early 1990s, when our current afterschool movement gained substantive ground, it had its own Achilles' heel. For example, commentators were apt to note the movement's marginality when compared to the institution of schooling, its loose and motley collection of approaches, its poor to nonexistent funding base, its overreliance on volunteers and an itinerate and paraprofessional teaching staff. Yet, if the programs described in this book can be taken as a serious indication, the current afterschool field has begun to mature, and startlingly so. Its new maturity includes an increasingly sophisticated reliance on generative theories and best teaching practices, and most remarkably, an ability to create productive spaces for learning that can often complement and, better yet, sometimes exceed what can be found in those schools negatively impacted by curricular constraints and of course unequal resources. These strengths can be traced in part to the leadership and sponsorship of agencies such as the Robert Bowne Foundation, which has funded research and publication, and The After-School Corporation, which has led through its large-scale orchestration of infrastructure and funding for afterschool programs in New York City. In addition, universities and academic communities have shown substantive parallel interest and support in recent years; scholars from a variety of disciplines have engaged in documenting, theorizing, and supporting out-of-school, alternative learning spaces (cf. Cole, 2006; Harkavy & Puckett, 1994; Heath, 2000, 2001; Vasquez, 2002). I believe that we should all stand wistful and admiring, to paraphrase Ralph Waldo Emerson, before what has been accomplished, as we also peer somewhat anxiously toward a future in which the current world of afterschool programs faces serious challenges to its still nascent identity.

The chapters in this book are, in fact, organized to reveal the ways in which the current afterschool movement can keep its balance while straddling competing educational approaches and ideologies: on one hand, standards-based reform and the policies associated with No Child Left Behind, which in practice have come to privilege accountability and high stakes testing and, on the other, practices and principles associated with the approach called "youth development," which interests itself not in academic achievement narrowly conceived, but in a broader conception of human development that includes social, artistic, civic, emotional, and intellectual growth. It is safe to say that many afterschool programs, given the informal association of people, activities, and collaborators that they still generally represent, have not thoroughly examined or articulated their theoretical and policy-related underpinnings in such a precise way. Indeed, one of the achievements of Hill's edited volume is to propose and enact such an approach as a model for the field. To be sure, the possibility of a hybrid model for the afterschool movement, one that can successfully serve two masters with integrity, becomes all the more important as pressures intensify to bring afterschool programs under the structural umbrella of school-day programming and, indeed, to evaluate them according to their success in contributing to our government's primary goal of increasing academic achievement for all children as measured by standardized tests. The rub is that the ideologies and practices of afterschool programs have long leaned toward the principles of youth development, even when those principles and their theoretical allegiances have not been explicitly articulated. To redirect all or most of their energies toward academic achievement, especially when such achievement is narrowly prescribed in terms of teaching methods and student outcomes, would be a wrenching shift for most in the afterschool world. I suggest that it would ultimately be a harmful one for schools and school-based goals as well and, in fact, for all those who worry about the economic and social futures of our citizenry.

To read the chapters in Hill's edited volume is to notice that the descriptions seem first of all to exemplify good teaching such as might occur anywhere—not just after school. We are presented with sound educational endeavors that not only respond sensitively and inventively to children's interests, needs, and predilections but also extend their knowledge, skills, and understanding into new domains. In some cases, the programs are conceived as ways to fill institutional gaps, providing occasions for learning that aren't always possible during a school day that is increasingly structured and scripted. McVarish (this volume), for instance, introduces us to In Addition, an afterschool program for elementary school students that is beautifully aligned with progressive recommendations for mathematics reform: an emphasis on collaboration and communities of learners, "real-life" problem-based activities, and an attention to conceptual understanding as well as procedural knowledge. In another and better age, the same activities and participant structures as we see after school through In Addition would take place during the school day.

Other afterschool classes in Hill's book unabashedly offer programming that doesn't usually find a place in the traditional academic curriculum. For example, Khurana (this volume) describes one such program that centered on the creation of comics, teaching us how activities such as drawing, inking, writing, and storyboarding, animated by participation in a popular cultural practice, provided the occasion for powerful identity work and skill building on the part of urban teenagers. In such an afterschool world, youth who do not flourish during school-based literacy activities can nonetheless experience the power of representing self, others, and community through the intersection of language and image—a skill set, by the way, increasingly recognized as the literacy of the future by theorists (Kress, 2003) and policy makers (Partnership for 21st Century Learning Skills, 2007) who are on the cutting edge. Interestingly, regardless of how explicitly the afterschool programs in this volume connect themselves with a school-day curriculum, they nonetheless could be conceptualized as addressing many state academic standards, as each chapter demonstrates in some detail. This fact should give us heart, suggesting that youth are daily engaged, or could easily be, in productive learning and doing of the sort we value, whether or not this occurs as a function of a formal standards-based curriculum.

The ease with which it seems possible to connect afterschool learning to school-based standards, as exemplified in this edited volume, should not, however, lull us into a fateful complacency. The move in U.S. educational policy, now well afoot, to make afterschool programming and out-of-school time a mere extension of the current school day, pressed into the service of academic achievement as determined almost exclusively through standardized tests, is not in my view a wise or defensible direction. In California, for example, afterschool is now increasingly labeled "extended day" programming, while funding sources from the state, passed through from the federal government, increasingly prescribe the nature of what happens during afterschool time, connecting it more and more directly to the school-day curriculum. More alarming still, with the state and federal money available in California, primarily through Proposition 49, a measure passed in 2002, and 21st Century Learning Center funding, comes the pressure to evaluate the effectiveness of afterschool programs, primarily through the collection of data that show an improvement in academic performance via school-day standardized test scores. Sometimes, additional testing is even required as part of the afterschool program itself.

Never mind that persistent and long-standing academic achievements gaps have not appreciably narrowed through the doing of traditional school. Never mind that underfunded, time-strapped afterschool programs are being asked to show a value added and to achieve results that the entire school day hasn't been able to accomplish. Never mind that afterschool programs are increasingly being evaluated largely on the basis of adding value to the goal of academic achievement, which draws them away from their historical strengths of ministering to the whole child and pulls them into an ever narrower focus on narrow notions of cognition. Never mind that the funding taken away from the actual delivery of programs and put toward the purpose of evaluations, which will likely show few if any gains, is funding that afterschool programs, already underfunded, can sorely afford to give up. Never mind that a veritable army of researchers and academics have long questioned, not the goals of No Child Left Behind, but the means used to achieve those goals, including testing children to death. The emperor is wearing no clothes, and it is long past time to say so.

I recently examined a reading test that a set of afterschool programs with which I am affiliated administered in an effort to satisfy current conceptions of rigorous evaluation and satisfactory program performance. In some ways, it is a sensible test, reasonably short and designed to be completed handily in the space of an hour or less, and, because it is a multiple-choice test, it is easily scored and certainly very familiar to youth in its format and textual expectations. The items on the test, now released to the public, were originally developed by a professional testing service. If its posttest companion shows an improvement in scores, then state administrators, university researchers, K–12 educators, and afterschool program directors and teachers will each sigh with relief and dance with joy, for here will be evidence that the program works in terms of improving the extremely important competencies of school-based reading comprehension and vocabulary development. Keep in mind, however, that the schools where many of our afterschool programs take place are ranked among the lowest scoring schools in the State of California in terms of the state's "academic performance index." Keep in mind, too, that the high schools have a devastatingly high dropout rate and that many youth have been disengaged from the pursuit of academics there for a distressingly long time. Keep in mind as well that the afterschool programs use media production as their enrichment centerpiece, more specifically digital storytelling and digital music, and that, when they are successful, they seem to be so because youth become deeply engaged in the opportunity to develop expertise around the creation of artifacts important in popular culture. It is certainly the case that youth acquire skills and knowledge through their participation in these media-intensive afterschool activities and that much of what they learn can be mapped onto state language arts standards. But it is not likely, I would wager, that the important things they have learned will position the eleventh graders, cognitively or dispositionally, to perform well on the afterschool test, that is, to read a passage from Nathaniel Hawthorne about how Young Goodman Brown "came forth at sunset into the street at Salem village" to inform his wife that his trip into the forest "must needs be done 'twixt now and sunrise." What they learn will likely not position them to be able to correctly answer, or to be interested in correctly answering, a multiple-choice question on the symbolic function of the forest during the American colonial period.

Let me be clear that this is absolutely not to say that youth aren't capable of correctly answering questions about, or couldn't acquire an appreciation of, or even should be assumed not to currently possess an interest in the themes of "Young Goodman Brown." It is to say, with some alarm, that afterschool programs serve as lifelines to many young people who are disengaged with traditional school, or in grave danger of becoming so, and that, to turn afterschool into more standard school—especially through the imposition of participant structures, textual practices, and tests that are themselves superficially connected to the very important social practices, skills and knowledge, and identities that youth are acquiring through, for example, an innovative program on fashion design (Thompson, this volume)—is to welcome the gathering of an ominous storm.

If, as I am arguing, afterschool programs should be loosed from strictures merely to duplicate school and to be evaluated on that basis, then it is fair to ask what functions they might alternately serve and what kind of research might document their achievements. It is also important to ask why and how such programs might be seen as contributing to the solution of the pressing issues that Kirsch and colleagues (2007) outline. The youth development literature offers one set of useful perspectives on these questions, and the chapters in this book offer a fine set of actual examples.

Mining these chapters for insights, and drawing as well on what I take to be central themes from sociocultural theorizing and research about literacy and learning in and out of school, I will briefly point to two past achievements and two future directions.

One achievement has to do with identity and agency. The chapters in this volume demonstrate again and again, within the contexts of the particular out-of-school time instructional programs herein described, that young people can and do develop senses of themselves as potent actors in their worlds, as people with skills and expertise and dispositions who can exert control over their educational, social, and even economic futures. "I feel like I have a special talent," exclaimed one young student full of her accomplishments in Fabulous Fashions (Thompson, this volume) and already envisioning a future career. "It was cool to test the water and the temperature," explained a burgeoning scientist who was also a fifth-grade participant in the afterschool Science Mentoring Project (Fancsali, this volume). "I think that I am more likely to speak about controversial things in class. More likely to help other people," volunteered a teenager who'd participated in an urban debate league (Hall, this volume) and whose newly developed sense of civic responsibility impels action and involvement. Indeed, some of the authors write explicitly in their chapters about identity formation. Khurana (this volume), for example, recounts how young people participating in the creation of comics took full advantage of the opportunity to explore issues related to gender, race, class, and other identity categories through their creation of characters whose struggles and triumphs paralleled their own.

The term "identity" often conjures up notions of crisis, even *sturm und drang* where adolescents are concerned, or it strikes one as an impossibly abstract notion to get hold of, being vaguely associated with a sense of self or sets of changing affiliations. Yet, concepts of identity and agency have emerged as central foci of research on activity and learning outside the classroom or apart from formal schooling, and identity is a leitmotif as well for a great deal of research and theorizing in the social sciences over the last twenty-five years. I would submit that a major accomplishment of many afterschool programs is their success in fostering among their constituents positive, agentive senses of self in relation to school, subject matters, careers, and abilities. It is useful to conceptualize identity as including interpersonal, epistemic, and discursive aspects (cf. Holland, Lachicotte, Skinner, & Cain, 1998; Hull & Greeno, 2006). Interpersonally, a person's identity includes his or her interactions with other people, including commitments and the ways in which the person is entitled, expected, and obligated to treat other people. Epistemically, a person's identity includes his or her interactions with the subject-matter contents of activities, including the ways he or she is committed, entitled, expected, and obligated to have and seek knowledge and understanding and to use the contents of a subject-matter domain. Discursively, contexts of identity afford models of self and opportunities to enact and represent a self.

I suspect that the best afterschool programs, like the best schools, privilege the construction of powerful identities and that successful learning and doing result from participation in activities that students invest with their identities. Such investment may occur for different reasons and combinations of reasons: the involvement of role models and experts from the local community and beyond (Fancsali, Hall, Khurana, McVarish, and Thompson, this volume); the opportunity to participate in valued cultural practices (Edwards, Khurana, and Thompson, this volume); the support and participation of parents and other significant adults and peers (Fancsali, Hall, McVarish, and Thompson, this volume); the chance to envision a future or future career (Fancsali, Khurana, and Thompson, this volume); opportunities to experience the acquisition of true expertise (Fancsali, Hall, Khurana, and McVarish, this volume); the situating of skills development within activities that have a larger purpose (Edwards, Fancsali, Hall, Khurana, and McVarish, this volume); and the engagement of multiple modalities in learning (Edwards, Fancsali, Hall, Khurana, McVarish, and Thompson, this volume). It is interesting to consider why some afterschool programs may be likelier places for students to invest activities with their identities than are some schools. And it is crucial to consider how afterschool programs and schools can partner so as to take advantage of afterschool's potential leadership in this regard. At this historical moment, most schools may appear best equipped to promote, test, and certify mastery, while some afterschool programs may seem more appropriate contexts for the development of interpersonal, epistemic, and discoursal identities.

A second achievement of afterschool programs, also aptly demonstrated in this volume, is the use of multiple modalities for learning and doing. It is noteworthy that in each of the programs described, children engaged in activities that drew on several senses and multiple modes of representation. Further, reading and language-based texts were often accompanied by, or sometimes even subordinate to, other symbolic systems—image, music, sound, movement. At the Fabulous Fashions afterschool program, participants searched the Internet for articles and images; imagined and sketched possible designs; touched, manipulated, cut, and sewed fabric; and finally strutted and strolled down the fashion runway (Thompson, this volume). During an out-of-school reading and writing workshop that focused on "doing hair," African American girls did indeed read aloud and write journals, but they also alternated roles as "hairstylists, clients, fashion critics, talkers, and listeners" (Edwards, this volume). At their Science Mentoring Project, children graphed air and water temperature, to be sure, but they also set traps for fish and performed a "plankton tow" (Fancsali, this volume). Movement is key in these programs as well—children move about and playfully romp, to be sure, but they learn to animate their bodies as models, debaters, and scientists too. Perhaps the philosopher Sheets-Johnstone (1998) is correct in arguing that "movement is at the root of our sense of agency and the generative source of our notions of space and time" (p. xv). (Compare Katz, 2007.)

Anthropologist Ruth Finnegan (2002) reminds us, and these chapters illustrate, that "human beings . . . use a vast range of communicative modes" (p. 223). Finnegan describes humans' communicative resources as encompassing "their powers of eye and ear and movement, their embodied interactions in and with the external environment, their capacities to interconnect along auditory, visual, tactile and perhaps olfactory modalities, and their ability to create and manipulate objects in the world" (p. 243). Finnegan does *not* argue that some people are good with some modes and not others—that there is a visual intelligence as opposed to a kinesthetic one, for example—but that a characteristic of human beings is employing the range. The importance of integrating learning and doing, and thereby allowing for a fuller play of communicative and representational modes, has of course long been a staple of progressive educational theory (e.g., Dewey, 1916/1966). However, with crises of funding, achievement, and accountability, schools have increasingly lost the opportunity to educate through arts and athletics. And with the long dominance of written language as both the means and product of schooling—some would say with our "logocentric bias"—it has not been customary for schools to value multiple modalities for self-expression, knowledge creation, and communication. Enter afterschool, right on time, marching in step with new digital technologies that increasingly make multimodality the *sine qua non* of communication (cf. Hull & Nelson, 2006).

Whether afterschool programs will continue to lead in terms of being positive settings for identity formation and multimodal learning of course depends on many things, but particularly on whether funding comes to be increasingly tied to the demonstration of improved academic performance during the school day. Toward that end, I suggest two new directions. First, it seems crucially important that afterschool programs be able and be allowed to document what they contribute to children's cognitive, affective, artistic, and social development, and concomitantly, that notions of research expand beyond program evaluation to include demonstrations of children's learning. As realizations of what children need to know and be able to do expand beyond the fundamental and the basic (Partnership for 21st Century Skills, 2007) and as schools and afterschools alike turn their efforts toward fostering attitudes, dispositions, skills, and knowledge that truly add value to individuals' and societies' futures in the new century, there will be a need as well to understand the role that afterschools can play in relation to schools and vice versa. This understanding will come through research that isn't put in a straightjacket through requirements that it use control groups, consist primarily of quantitative data, or be conducted by "third-party" or external evaluators. More positively put, it will assess learning via a range of alternative methods both under development and yet to be imagined, it will engage program staff in contributing to the documentation of that learning, and it will chart the rocky terrain of institutional contexts. I expect, then, that future collections on afterschool programs will include not only descriptions of successful practices and conflict-free organizations but also accounts of the particular struggles—political, economic, ideological, epistemological—that will be a permanent fixture on the school and afterschool educational landscapes. In the current volume, McVarish allows us to glimpse that terrain when she describes how the In Addition mathematics program almost lost its clientele to a requirement, imposed by the schools, for test preparation after school, but crafted a solution by persuading and supporting parents to themselves assume greater responsibility for ensuring that children were ready to face and conquer their achievement tests. More accounts like this, more ethnographically textured and nuanced, will be paramount as we confront and negotiate unhelpful policies and reimagine and transform institutional relationships.

Afterschool programs are local phenomena, growing from the needs and strengths of local communities. But if anything characterizes our global world, it is the way in which we are interconnected. Appadurai (1996) describes how both texts and people are mobile, flowing across national borders and geographies through the migration of people and the flows of images and texts through media and the Internet. To be sure, ours is an age in which our interconnected world grows ever more salient, even as we become increasingly aware of our own identities as multiple, and increasingly required to participate in the imagined realities of others. The current movement to characterize twenty-first century skills importantly includes "global awareness" as core (Partnership for 21st Century Skills, 2007). It is interesting to consider, then, how afterschool programs can contribute in this regard, prompting young people's developing senses of themselves in relation to others to include understandings of different cultures, traditions, languages, and ideologies, both those within the United States and those outside it.

Historically in the United States, the institution of the school has shown itself remarkably capable of assimilating and transforming innovation. In his examination of the expansion of the high school during the early twentieth century and the move later on to retract its services in favor of a focus on the "basics," Tyack (1979) notes, "School systems then, as now, had a considerable capacity to respond to lay criticism by incorporating certain changes into the system and then transforming them into innocuous and smoothly running parts of the pedagogical machinery" (p. 52). On the other hand, at least in their most interesting and powerful incarnations, out-of-school programs originate to and can fill important gaps in school-based services, often in relation to particular skills, subject matters, activities, or educational philosophies, and almost always for excluded, neglected, or disenfranchised groups. I think of the Freedom Schools that flourished as a centerpiece of the civil rights movement in Mississippi during the 1960s as a short-lived but durable and inspiring reminder of such purposes. As Perlstein (1990) explains, these Freedom Schools "offered young black Mississippians an education that public schools would not supply, one that both provided intellectual stimulation and linked learning to participation in the movement to transform the South's segregated society" (p. 297). The question of the moment is whether the current afterschool movement can be successful, in the face of rising economic and ideological pressures fueled by legislative mandates, in maintaining what can be most powerful about its role. History would not make us optimistic, but the accounts in this book renew our energy and our hope.

References

Appadurai, A. (1996). *Modernity at large: Cultural dimensions of globalization.* Minneapolis: University of Minnesota Press.

Cole, M. (2006). *The fifth dimension: An after-school program built on diversity.* New York: Russell Sage.

Dewey, J. (1966). *Democracy and education: An introduction to the philosophy of education.* New York: Free Press. (Original work published 1916)

Finnegan, R. (2002). *Communicating: The multiple modes of human interconnection.* London: Routledge.

Gee, J. P. (1996). *Social linguistics and literacies: Ideology in discourses* (2nd ed.). London: Falmer Press.

Halpern, R. (2004). *Confronting the big lie: The need to reframe expectations of afterschool programs.* Chicago: Partnership for After School Education.

Harkavy, I., & Puckett, J. L. (1994). Lessons from Hull House for the contemporary urban university. *Social Service Review, 28*(3), 299–321.

Heath, S. B. (2000). Seeing our way into learning. *Cambridge Journal of Education, 30*(1): 121–132.

Heath, S. B. (2001). Three's not a crowd: Plans, roles and focus in the arts. *Educational Researcher, 30*(7), 10–17.

Holland, D., Lachicotte, W., Jr., Skinner, D., & Cain, C. (1998). *Identity and agency in cultural worlds.* Cambridge, MA: Harvard University Press.

hooks, bell. (1989). *Talking back: Thinking feminist, thinking black.* Boston: South End Press.

Hull, G., & Greeno, J. (2006). Identity and agency in non-school and school worlds. In Z. Bekerman, N. C. Burbules, & D. Silberman-Keller (Eds.), *Learning in places: The informal education reader* (pp. 77–97). New York: Peter Lang.

Hull, G., & Schultz, K. (Eds.). (2002). *School's out! Bridging out-of-school literacies with classroom practice.* New York: Teachers College Press.

Katz, M.-L. (2007). *Growth in motion: Documenting how young women's embodied identity, cognitive development and academic success are supported through participation in dance after-school. Final Report to the Robert Bowne Foundation.* (Available from the Robert Bowne Foundation, 55 Water Street, New York, NY 10041-0006)

Kirsch, I., Braun, H., Yamamoto, K., & Sum, A. (2007). *America's perfect storm: Three forces changing our nation's future.* Princeton, NJ: Educational Testing Service.

Kress, G. (2003). *Literacy in the new media age.* London: Routledge.

Partnership for 21st Century Learning Skills. (2007). [Home page]. Retrieved March 20, 2007, from http://www.21stcenturyskills.org

Perlstein, D. (1990). Teaching freedom: SNCC and the creation of the Mississippi Freedom Schools. *History of Education Quarterly, 30*(3), 297–324.

Rogoff, B. (2003). *The cultural nature of human development.* New York: Oxford University Press.

Sheets-Johnstone, M. (1998). *The primacy of movement.* Philadelphia: John Benjamins.

Street, B. V. (1995). *Social literacies: Critical approaches to literacy in development, ethnography and education.* London: Longman.

Tyack, D. B. (1979). The high school as a social service agency: Historical perspectives on current policy issues. *Educational Evaluation and Policy Analysis, 1*(5), 45–57.

Vasquez, O. (2002). *La Clase Magica: Imagining optimal possibilities in a bilingual community of learners.* Mahwah, NJ: Lawrence Erlbaum Associates.

Preface

BACKGROUND

Whether held in schools, community centers, churches, or other neighborhood institutions, Out-of-School Time (OST) programs are increasing in number (Bodilly & Beckett, 2005; Fashola, 2002). OST programs are offered in a variety of formats, including afterschool, summertime, and, occasionally, programs held before school. They are increasingly looked upon to bridge achievement gaps between youth in low-income communities with failing schools and students from more affluent communities (Lauver, Little, & Weiss, 2004). This trend has been amplified by the introduction of No Child Left Behind legislation and high-stakes testing, which has put increasing pressure on low performing out-of-school time programs to focus on academic achievement (Halpern, 2002).

Claiming unrealistic expectations given the limited funding, some OST programs have attempted to resist this pressure through advocacy and public education and policy efforts. Others have, rather than lose funding and close their doors, adapted to the academic mandates. Still others have attempted to achieve a balance between the academic needs of youth and their other developmental needs. This tension can be translated into a struggle over identity—whether the "boundary between the in-school day and the out-of-school hours should be blurred or erased" (Heath, 2001, p. 15).

OST programs that merely mirror the school day or drill students on test-taking skills do not necessarily improve young people's academic performance. National funders and policy makers have recognized that quality afterschool programs are not "just more school" or mere extensions of the school day (Stonehill, 2006; Wright, 2005). Evaluations of OST programs—for example, those conducted by the Mathematica Policy Institute of the 21st Century Community Learning Centers, a federally funded OST program (James-Burdumy, Dynarski, Moore, Deke, & Mansfield, 2005), and the Massachusetts After-School Research Study (MARS, 2005)—have mixed findings regarding the causal link between academic achievement and youth participating in OST programs. The conclusion by the MARS study is that "it is not clear that expecting programs to have direct academic effects is a fruitful avenue for the afterschool field" (MARS, 2005, p. 2). Indeed, OST programs may help the development of "prerequisites" (Miller, 2003) for academic success, with the outcomes determined by longer range measures, such as high school completion rates (Kaufman, 2006).

Other evaluations of OST programs have found some positive impacts on student achievement, but the programs do not have to focus on academics to do so (Lauver et al., 2004). Rather, programs that are flexible, taking into account youth interests and needs, are much more effective at attracting and retaining young people as well as supporting their academic achievement. This support can be accomplished with a wide range of OST program models, including those that incorporate high-interest activities such as sports, the arts, and youth leadership.

Why Write This Book?

While there is currently pressure on OST programs by school administration as well as funders to bridge the achievement gap, OST programs are seldom provided with adequate resources or training to either "resist the pressure" to become more like school (Halpern, 2002) or to infuse academics in ways appropriate to the OST context (which, historically, have not had academics as their focus). While staff at OST programs recognize that programs don't work if they are "just more school," they are often ill-prepared to both create an environment that demonstrates the best of youth development as well as align themselves with learning standards in an effort to support youth academically. The difficulty of achieving this dual goal is understandable when one considers that youth development involves addressing the full range of social, cognitive, emotional, artistic, and civic competencies (Delgado, 2002). (See the next section on the framework for youth development.) Youth themselves say that they come to OST programs primarily to socialize with friends and engage in fun activities, and the MARS report confirms that youth engagement is a key element in retaining youth as well as contributing to positive outcomes (MARS, 2005). On the other hand, parents, particularly in low-income neighborhoods, say they want OST programs to provide academic support and homework help (Duffet, et al. 2004).

These competing agendas create a challenge to the youth development field: How to create a "space between fun and school" (Hull, 2004), to capture the imaginations of youth, yet respond to their pressing academic needs. This book was written to help reconcile these competing agendas and to provide guidance for OST program design.

The Importance of OST Staff

The quality of OST staff, reflected in their training, degrees, and certification, is a key component in quality afterschool programs. According to the MARS study, "better paid and better trained staff spend more quality activity time with children, which is the single most important factor in the success of an after-school program" (MARS, 2005, p. 23). Yet professional development in the OST field, whether preservice or inservice, has been sketchy at best, and nonexistent in many cases. There is a need to provide training, materials, and program models to help OST staff better design quality programs.

OST programs and staff, particularly from community organizations, such as churches and youth centers, are often successful in engaging youth during the out-of-school time. They have a long history of offering engaging, high interest activities such as sports, arts, and youth leadership. Many of these programs and activities are firmly grounded in principles of youth development. The staff is often intimately familiar with the community, having known and created relationships with children and families over the course of many years. These staff members falter, however, when required to design programs that support academic achievement. Indeed, many of the activities they *already* are offering support academic learning standards, yet they are unaware of how the activities do so. If staff were more aware of the possibilities and range of models, their current activities could easily be tweaked or modified to become more powerful supports to academic achievement.

Conversely, school-based personnel, such as public school teachers, because of an influx of funding, are newly charged with designing after-school programs. Staff may be very skilled in curriculum design and lesson planning and have an intimate knowledge of students' academic needs. School staff get it wrong by recreating an environment during the afterschool time that does not diverge, in any meaningful way, from school. Activities are often narrowly focused on remediation and test preparation. And yet, why would more of the same—activities that have not necessarily succeeded during the school day—succeed *after* school? This limited view of programming during the out-of-school time results in participants who "vote with their feet" and in dismal retention rates, particularly for older youth (Lauver et al., 2004).

THE PURPOSE OF THIS BOOK

The purpose of this book is to provide rich, in-depth descriptions, written by individual practitioners, of promising OST programs. These programs attempt to achieve, and in many cases are successful in achieving, a delicate balance—they are neither mere extensions of the school day nor programs that ignore students' academic needs, particularly those of struggling youth. The book presents OST programs that emphasize and address the multiple needs of youth: They are programs that offer youth the opportunity to develop their academic, social, physical, emotional, civic, and artistic competencies. The program descriptions are not meant to appear flawless; the authors very often share both their challenges and successes in designing and sustaining their particular OST program. In doing so, they provide a realistic picture of the many ways OST programs struggle with, and sometimes can succeed in, serving youth.

You will note that none of these programs claims to produce outcomes such as increased test scores or higher report card grades. This is primarily because, while showing promise, the programs have not been evaluated based on the criterion of academic achievement. As mentioned earlier, studies have shown the mixed results of OST programs in terms of short-term academic outcomes. Documenting the outcomes of youth participation in these programs may be something more suited to longitudinal studies, which may look at longer term indicators of achievement, such as high school completion rates. In addition, limiting the measure of program success to academic achievement ignores outcomes that are much more difficult to measure, such as increased self-efficacy and a vision for the future. Studies are needed that can document growth in these types of competencies, as well as account for a range of complex variables that affect academic achievement, such as afterschool child care responsibilities and employment.

The programs documented in this book were purposefully selected using a set of criteria including the following:

- The programs are held in a range of contexts: either in schools during the out-of-school time or in a community organization, such as a community center;
- The OST instructors come from a range of backgrounds: in some cases, they are university professors and graduate students; in some cases, they are artists, scientists, or professional fashion designers; and, in yet other cases, they are teachers from the school day who are working in the afterschool program.

The programs that satisfied the above criteria were further worthy of mention in this book because they

a. Are well-designed and innovative, aligning activities that support positive youth development alongside of learning standards.

b. Retain youth, particularly older youth, in OST programs, at a time when young people have many competing interests.

c. Are examples of ways to successfully integrate multiple institutions—schools, universities, and community-based organizations as well as parents and youth—in productive partnerships.

AUDIENCE FOR THIS BOOK

This book was written for OST practitioners, managers as well as front line staff. This includes schoolteachers who work in OST programs, perhaps as a second job. The intended audience also includes youth development specialists, teaching artists, and other professionals who work in youth centers and community-based organizations. Finally, the audience for this book includes principals and executives and managers of community-based organizations. We hope that the audience for the book will learn from and adapt these models as they create their own OST programs or revise and improve their current programs.

HOW THE BOOK IS ORGANIZED

Each chapter in this book is written by a different author, describing a different OST program. Because they are written by different authors, the reader will hear a distinct "voice" and tone to each chapter. This diversity of voice, we believe, is a positive aspect of the book, and one that makes it a compelling story. In fact, we believe that diversity is probably a common, and unifying, strand across OST programs. While we can also identify other common patterns of promising OST programs, a "cookie cutter" approach is most likely to their detriment. We believe that, rather than making programs all look and operate the same, diversity should be celebrated.

Each chapter presents a different program model, describing a different approach to OST program activity. The focus of the programs is wide—from cartooning to math. Some of the program activities appear "school-like," and some activities may, on the surface, look merely artistic or recreational. Yet, the school-like activities are firmly based in Youth Development principles, and, embedded within the recreational or arts activities are strategies that ultimately support youth's academic achievement and are aligned with state learning standards.

As mentioned, even though programs described in each chapter may be quite different, it is possible to identify an overarching, or common, set of principles, and basic assumptions. First, the programs were all designed with sensitivity to high-interest activities that are based on student interests with the intention of encouraging youth participation. In addition, the programs are designed to support Youth Development competencies as well as learning standards. Finally, the programs encourage students to draw from the community as well as each other as resources to support learning.

Each chapter is followed by a section on replication ideas. Please note that even though programs can't be transported, in whole, to a different context, they can be adopted to different program contexts and audiences. The diversity of programs should be encouraged—we encourage the replication of a range of program applications, as long as they adhere to a set of common principles. Finally, each chapter is followed by a list of references and resources to help the practitioner develop knowledge of the program and area of expertise.

References

Bodilly, S., & Beckett, M. K. (2005). *Making out of school time matter: Evidence for an action agenda*. Santa Monica, CA: Rand Corporation.

Delgado, M. (2002). *New frontiers for youth development in the twenty-first century.* New York: Teachers College Press.

Duffet, A., Johnson, J., Farkas, S., Kung, S., & Ott, A. (2004). *All work and no play? Listening to what kids and parents really want from out-of-school time.* New York: Public Agenda. (Paper commissioned by the Wallace Foundation)

Fashola, O. S. (2002). *Building effective afterschool programs.* Thousand Oaks, CA: Corwin Press.

Halpern, R. (2002). A different kind of child development institution: The history of after-school programs for low-income children. *Teachers College Record, 104*(2), 178–211.

Heath, S. B. (2001). Three's not a crowd: Plans, roles, and focus in the arts. *Educational Researcher, 30*(7), 10–17.

Hull, G. (2004). Personal communication.

James-Burdumy, S., Dynarski, M., Moore, M., Deke, J., & Mansfield, W. (2005). *When schools stay open late: The national evaluation of the 21st Century Community Learning Centers Program.* Washington, DC: U.S. Department of Education, Institute of Education Sciences, National Center for Education Evaluation and Regional Assistance. Retrieved March 20, 2007, from http://www.ed.gov/ies/ncee

Kaufman, B. (2006). Personal communication.

Lauver, S., Little, P., & Weiss, H. (2004, July). *Moving beyond the barriers: Attracting and sustaining youth participation in out-of-school time programs* (Issues and Opportunities in Out-of-School Time Evaluation Brief No. 6). Cambridge, MA: Harvard Family Research Project.

Massachusetts After-School Research Study (MARS). (2005). *Pathways to success for youth: What counts in after-school.* Boston, MA: United Way of Massachusetts Bay.

Miller, B. M. (2003). *Critical hours: Afterschool programs and educational success.* Quincy, MA: Nellie Mae Education Foundation. Retrieved March 19, 2007, from http://www.nmefdn.org/uploads/Critical_Hours.pdf

Stonehill, R. (2006). The future of federal afterschool initiatives [Interview]. *SEDL Letter, 18*(1), 15–16.

Wright, E. (2005). *Supporting student success: A governor's guide to extra learning opportunities.* Washington, DC: National Governors Association Center for Best Practices.

Acknowledgments

Sara L. Hill, Editor

I would like to first acknowledge Lena Townsend, Executive Director of the Robert Bowne Foundation and Jennifer Stanley, President of the Board of Directors of the Robert Bowne Foundation. This work could not, literally, have been possible if it weren't for their vision, leadership, and support.

I would also like to acknowledge Jan Gallagher of Gallagher Communications, editor of the journal *Afterschool Matters.* Jan did the initial editing on articles and reports that formed the basis of chapters in this book. Her brilliant editing work allowed me to have a much easier time with the current work at hand.

Finally, I would like to thank my husband, Michael Winkler, as well as our children, Keiko, Makoto, and Daniel. They are the sails and rudder on the sailboat of my life.

Daneell Edwards, Contributing Author

I would like to thank Sara Hill at the Robert Bowne Foundation for her reviews and insightful comments throughout this book project. I also would like to thank the young ladies in the afterschool program for allowing me to be their "hair teacher."

Cheri Fancsali, Contributing Author

My thanks to the teachers, students, and mentors who participated in the Science Mentoring Project on which my chapter is based. I also thank the researchers who conducted this study and the Robert Bowne Foundation and the National Science Foundation for their support.

Georgia Hall, Contributing Author

I wish to thank Impact Coalition, Will Baker, students and coaches of the New York Urban Debate League, the Baltimore Urban Debate League, and the Boston Debate League for their contributions to this chapter. This chapter is adapted from a paper originally funded by the Robert Bowne Foundation.

Sarita Khurana, Contributing Author

I would like to thank Alex Simmons and the students in The Art of Making Comics afterschool class during the spring 2004 semester at School of the Future. Thanks go also to the Robert Bowne Foundation for supporting this research and writing with their fellowship and, in particular, to Sara Hill and my fellow 2003–2004 Bowne research fellows, who provided a community and context for this writing. Thanks to The Educational Alliance; to Mitzi Sinnott, who directed the afterschool program at the time of this research; and, finally, to my mentor and friend, Rosa Agosto, for her commitment to young people and the ongoing inspiration she provides.

Judith McVarish, Contributing Author

I wish to thank the students, parents, and faculty team of the In Addition afterschool program. Their energy, dedication, and curiosity supplied the material for this narration.

Anne L. Thompson, Contributing Author

I would like to thank the young women at the middle school, whose hard work and enthusiasm inspired this chapter. If they can maintain the passion and dedication they put into fashion design, they will achieve great things in life. I would also like to acknowledge the Sports & Arts in Schools Foundation, which introduced me to the afterschool world and allowed me enough flexibility to have three children and keep working in the field I love. A very special note of appreciation goes to Jim O'Neill, who gave me a chance to run my first afterschool program, and who has remained immensely supportive over the years. Also, this chapter would not have been possible without Sara Hill who was tireless in her work on this book and a top-notch editor. Finally, I would like to thank my husband, Steve Madden, and Luke, Christine, and Catherine, who allowed me time out of our hectic family life to work on this project.

Publisher's Acknowledgments

Corwin Press gratefully acknowledges the contributions of the following individuals:

Joseph Cronin, President, EDVISORS
Braintree, MA

Darin S. Drill, Principal, Cascade High School
Turner, OR

Jane Kerschner, Director of School Programs, The Ophelia Project®
Erie, PA

Priscilla M. Little, Associate Director,
Harvard Family Research Project, Cambridge, MA

Jerry Vaughn, Principal
Central Elementary School, Cabot, AR

Paul Young, Executive Director
West After School Center, Inc., Lancaster, OH

About the Editor

 **Sara L. Hill, EdD,** has worked in community-based education for twenty years. She has conducted research at community-based youth programs, both in the United States as well as internationally, and published several articles in the areas of literacy, youth development, and community-based education. She received her MEd from the Harvard Graduate School of Education, and her EdD from Peabody College, Vanderbilt University.

About the Contributors

Daneell Edwards is a doctoral candidate in the Language, Literacy, and Culture Program in the Teaching and Learning Department at Peabody College, Vanderbilt University. Her research interests include the history of African American literacy education, contemporary African American adolescents, African American language, literacy practices, embodied practices, and cultural practices in out-of-school settings.

Cheri Fancsali, PhD, is a senior program officer in research and evaluation at the Academy for Educational Development (AED). At AED, she conducts evaluations of school- and community-based educational programs, especially those pertaining to teacher professional development, school reform, afterschool opportunities, and gender equity. Formerly, Fancsali was a special education and early childhood teacher. She has a PhD in sociology and education from Columbia University, where she also received her master's degree in educational policy.

Georgia Hall, PhD, has extensive experience as a researcher and evaluator of youth development and out-of-school time programs and practices. She recently completed serving as Research Scientist on the Massachusetts After-School Research Study, which was a statewide research study of 78 afterschool programs in Massachusetts. Other recent projects include evaluation of the national Discovering Community Initiative for which she produced "Discovering Community: Activities for Afterschool Programs," which is now being disseminated. Hall is currently the Principal Investigator for the Boston Public School's Out-of-Harm's Way Initiative. She recently completed coediting an issue of *New Directions for Youth Development* focusing on the transition of youth from adolescence to early adulthood. Georgia is an enthusiastic youth basketball and softball coach and was a member of her high school speech and debate club.

Glynda A. Hull is Professor of Language, Literacy, and Culture in the Graduate School of Education at the University of California, Berkeley.

Her research examines digital technologies and new literacies, adult literacy and changing contexts and requirements for work, writing and students at risk, and community/school/university partnerships. A recent book is *School's Out! Bridging Out-of-School Literacies with Classroom Practice* (written with Katherine Schultz and published by Teachers College Press). She is cofounder of DUSTY (Digital Underground Storytelling for Youth), a community technology center in Oakland, CA, where she designs and studies afterschool programs on literacy and multimodal composing for children and adults.

Sarita Khurana received her master's degree from the Harvard Graduate School of Education, Risk and Prevention Program. She also does consulting work with youth development organizations, media arts programs, and schools, and she is a filmmaker. She directed *Bangla East Side,* a documentary about immigrant Bangladeshi youth growing up in the Lower East Side of New York City. She is currently working on another documentary film, *Personality,* about Bollywood backup dancers (to be released next year), and is in her first year of an MFA program in film at Columbia University.

Judith McVarish, PhD, is Assistant Professor of Mathematics Education at St. John's University. For over three decades, she has been in the mathematics education field, as a teacher, tutor, staff developer, and college professor. Her particular research interests include how teachers and students develop and assess their mathematics understanding and how the afterschool setting can be utilized to increase elementary students' mathematics engagement and learning. Recent publications have been focused in the areas of urban teacher beliefs about obstacles to effective mathematics teaching, self-assessment across disciplines, and how to help children develop the capacity to pose problems as well as solve them. She is Director of In Addition, a St. John's afterschool mathematics program, and author of *Infusing Mathematics Reasoning into Elementary School Classrooms* (New York: Routledge, forthcoming in spring 2007).

Anne L. Thompson is Director of Education and Research at New Jersey After 3, a statewide organization providing afterschool programming to children throughout New Jersey. Previously she was Director of Special Projects at the Sports & Arts in Schools Foundation, and she has also served as a consultant on afterschool issues to The After-School Corporation, the Children's Aid Society, and the Madison Square Garden's Cheering for Children Foundation. Before entering the afterschool field, she was a lawyer specializing in health care and mergers and acquisitions.

Introduction

Foundations Of Positive Youth Development

Sara L. Hill

RESILIENCY

Historically, research on low-income youth and families stemmed from a medical, "problem-focused approach" to research, focusing on "disease, illness, maladaptation, incompetence, deviance" (Benard, 1991, p. 1). Families and youth were viewed as problems that needed remediation (Heath & McLaughlin, 1993), and interventions were created as solutions to the problems. This approach was challenged by researchers who noticed in longitudinal studies of children growing up in environments such as war, genocide, abuse, and neglect that a surprisingly large number of children ended up as productive, healthy individuals rather than as what had been expected of them—i.e., drug-addicted, abusers, and worse (Benard, 1991, Werner & Smith, 1982).

The researchers identified a range of competencies and protective factors they attributed to what was called *resiliency*. Garmezy, Masten, and Tellegen (1984) noted that factors supporting resiliency tend to fall into three general categories: qualities of the child, characteristics of the family, and support from outside the family. Individual attributes and competencies were identified as

- *Social competence:* flexibility, empathy, caring, communication skills, a sense of humor, and other pro-social behavior.
- *Problem-solving skills:* ability to think abstractly, reflectively, and flexibly and to be able to attempt alternative solutions for both cognitive and social problems.

- *Autonomy:* a sense of one's own identity and an ability to act independently and exert some control over one's environment.
- *Sense of purpose and future:* healthy expectancies, goal-directedness, success orientation, achievement motivation, educational aspirations, persistence, hopefulness, and belief in a bright future. (Bernard, 1991, p. 7)

Protective factors in the environment (family, school, community) were also identified. These included

- *Caring and support:* The opportunity to establish a close bond with at least one person who provided them with stable care. In the community setting, this can include access to resources such as adequate childcare.
- *High expectations:* The belief that children can achieve and succeed, usually aligned with structure, discipline, and clear rules and regulations.
- *Opportunity to participate:* The opportunity to contribute and feel a valuable member of a group (Bernard, 1991).

Positive Youth Development

Resiliency theory became the basis of a philosophy of positive youth development. This framework, rather than starting with the deficits of youth, uses competencies and developmental assets as the baseline for thinking about young people's needs. It looks not only to the individual but also to the environment for factors that can either foster or hamper healthy development. While youth development can take place in a range of community settings, not every setting supports youth development (Delgado, 2002). Programs and services for youth that do not spring from a youth development perspective are usually geared narrowly toward intervention to prevent behaviors, such as teen pregnancy.

In the last twenty years, there has been a great deal of work on youth development, in particular the work of the Youth Development Institute of the Fund for the City of New York and the Search Institute.[1] These organizations have helped identify, articulate, and codify a set of principles and practices for youth development programming. They have identified youth development programs as those which are aimed toward broad-based, normative, developmental goals, and encompass outcomes such as the acquisition of social, emotional, civic, artistic, and intellectual competencies. Other features identified in youth development programming include a "sense of safety; challenging and interesting activities; sense of belonging; supportive relationships with adults; leadership; input and decision-making; and community service" (Gambone & Arbreton, 1997, p. 2).

---

[1] For more information, see www.fcny.org and www.search-institute.org.

WHAT ARE YOUTH DEVELOPMENT PROGRAMS?

Youth development programs in the United States have been around for at least a century, emerging in response to societal needs to address changing economic circumstances, such as the childcare needs of single parent families (Halpern, 2002). Programs have been held in a range of settings, including community centers, schools, churches, and ethnic clubs. They provide a variety of offerings, which may be grouped into broad categories including (1) performance and self-expression, (2) recreation, (3) self-enhancement, (4) educational enrichment and career exploration, (5) citizenship, and (6) comprehensive services (Merry, 2000, p. 27). These categories subsume activities such as graphic and visual arts, theater and dance, sports and athletics, community service and youth leadership, employment and training programs, and health care and mental health counseling. These programs have been aligned with school reform efforts (Cibulka & Kritek, 1996) and participation in Out-of-School Time (OST) programs has been associated with school success (Vandell & Lee, 1999).

Academic achievement has not, historically, been the preoccupation of OST programs. OST programs have, over the years, emphasized sports, arts, and leadership opportunities because they have a profound understanding of the needs of youth during the out-of-school time, as well as knowledge of what engages and draws youth to programs. Activities or projects at OST programs often involve the creation of end products, such as advocacy campaigns or theatrical productions, geared for wide audiences, including parents, other youth participants, funders, community residents, and government officials (Heath & McLaughlin, 1994; Merry, 2000).

While schools are the primary spaces where OST programs are now held, there is a long history of community-based organizations providing afterschool services. Community-based organizations are unique, and valuable, institutions, with the potential to establish "creative partnerships among education institutions, communities, and businesses" (Heath, 2001, p. 11). Community-based organizations, if utilized wisely, are a middle ground that can be an important vehicle linking school and home. They do so stemming from "traditions of community advocacy and organizing" (Hill, 2004), as well as by the fact that staff often come from the local community and have long-term relationships with children and families. There is a growing recognition of this important role, as the federal funding requires that schools have linkages with community-based organizations that are, in turn, contracted to provide services in schools.

Delgado (2002) conducted a comprehensive review of youth development theory and practice in an attempt to synthesize the range of understandings regarding what is, and isn't, a youth development program. He identified some salient features that can serve as a comprehensive and informative framework for designing and evaluating programs. According to Delgado, excellent youth development programs

- Deepen creativity, provide critical tools for negotiating developmental stages, and provide multiple avenues for the processing of cognitive information;
- Provide youth with opportunities to succeed and contribute to their community;
- Build on youth assets and what youth value;
- Have multiple clear, high, and realistic expectations for participants;
- Are voluntary and provide youth with decision-making powers in shaping programming (Delgado, 2002, p. 80).

LEARNING STANDARDS

Learning standards are key to school reform efforts. Standards-based reform is an approach to school improvement that states "plainly and clearly what results schools *should* produce and what skills and knowledge students *should* acquire as they pass through school" (Finn, Julian, & Petrilli, 2006, p. 8). That is, it is an approach where the success of a school is determined by its performance measured against "clear, commonly defined goals" (Schmoker & Marzano, 1999).

A slow groundswell over the past 20 years in the learning standards movement occurred as a result of several phenomena, beginning with the publication of *A Nation at Risk* (1983). The next major impetus came with the 1994 reauthorization of the Elementary and Secondary Education Act (ESEA) called the Improving America's Schools Act, as well as Congress's Goals 2000 Act, both federal incentives for standards-based reform. An additional pressure for reform came with the advent of No Child Left Behind (NCLB), which tied funding with school achievement outcomes. An additional impetus was fueled in part by federal law, passed in 1996, requiring states that receive federal Title 1 funds to develop standards.

As a result of this burgeoning legislation, states are now required to create and implement content standards and use them to guide school assessment. As of now, there is no nationwide set of standards, but national organizations such as the National Council of Teachers of Mathematics (NCTM) and National Council of Teachers of English (NCTE) have identified standards, which often serve as a template for state standards. There is almost a standards "overkill" situation, and there have been at least 200 identified standards (Marzano & Kendall, 1998). There is ongoing debate over how much time during the school day can be devoted to covering specific standards and whether the school day should be lengthened to do so.

Criticism has been leveled again "bad" standards, that is, standards that are too vague, which privilege skills over content (Finn et al., 2006). There have been calls for national standards and national tests aligned with standards. Several states, in response, have revised their standards to become more specific, calling them "academic content standards" and have worked toward curricula and assessments that are aligned with state standards. In addition, there are now clearinghouses, such as Mid-continent Research for Education and Learning (McREL[2]), which have collated states' standards and which provide additional resources as well as technical assistance and training in curricula-based standards.

Whether state-based or national, standards are here to stay and will be an ongoing presence in the lives of school districts, teachers, and children. Standards-based school reform is increasing in importance, particularly to school administrators, as schools are often approved or denied accreditation based on standards. As well, states are now developing and using academic content standards for a wide variety of evaluations and school improvement initiatives. For example, they are now used as the basis for end-of-course examinations at the high school level, for grade promotion in the elementary level, and to define the minimum skills needed to graduate from high school with a regular high school diploma (Rabinowitz, Roeber, Schroeder, & Sheinker, 2006).

Many OST programs currently offer activities that support academic outcomes which are aligned with state standards. These activities, however, are often wholly embedded. That is, they are not intentional—on the surface one cannot easily discern the ways that OST activities support learning standards. In addition, OST programs often do not do a good job of articulating to school personnel the value of their offerings or of demonstrating the ways that their activities support state standards. This has, at times, created a tension between school administration and OST programs, where the two institutions have similar goals yet do not fully understand each other's history and purpose. On the other hand, schools do not fully understand or utilize the range of community supports that can help them with their mission. A deeper understanding of the links between youth development, OST programs, and school success is needed for both schools and OST programs to achieve their goals.

This book will provide concrete models and a clear direction for how schools and OST programs can be natural partners in the effort to close the achievement gap. It will demonstrate how OST programs can further align their activities with learning standards, but in ways that are appropriate to their social and historical context—as youth development agencies.

References

Bernard, B. (1991). *Fostering resiliency in kids: Protective factors in the family, school and community*. Portland, OR: Western Regional Center for Drug-Free Schools and Communities.

---

[2] For more information, see www.mcrel.org.

Cibulka, J. G., & Kritek, W. J. (Eds.). (1996). *Coordination among schools, families, and communities: Prospects for educational reform.* Albany: State University of New York Press.

Delgado, M. (2002). *New frontiers for youth development in the twenty-first century.* New York: Teachers College Press.

Finn, C. E., Julian, L., & Petrilli, M. J. (2006). *2006 The State of State Standards.* Washington, DC: Thomas B. Fordham Foundation.

Gambone, M. A., & Arbreton, A. J. A. (1997). *Safe havens: The contributions of youth organizations to healthy adolescent development.* Philadelphia: Public/Private Ventures.

Garmezy, N., Masten, A. S., & Tellegen, A. (1984). The study of stress and competence in children: A building block for developmental psychopathology. *Child Development, 55,* 97–111.

Halpern, R. (2002). A different kind of child development institution: The history of after-school programs for low income children. *Teachers College Record, 104*(2), 178–211.

Heath, S. B. (2001, October). Three's not a crowd: Plans, roles, and focus in the arts. *Educational Researcher, 30*(7), 10–17.

Heath, S. B., & McLaughlin, M.W. (Eds.). (1993). *Identity and inner-city youth: Beyond ethnicity and gender.* New York: Teachers College, Columbia University.

Heath, S. B., & McLaughlin, M.W. (1994). Learning for anything everyday. *Journal of Curriculum Studies, 26*(5), 471–489.

Hill, S. (2004, Spring). Community-based youth organizations negotiating educational and social equity. *Afterschool Matters* (Occasional Paper No. 2). New York: The Robert Bowne Foundation.

Marzano, R. J., & Kendall, J. S. (1998). *Awash in a sea of standards.* Denver, CO: Mid-Continent Research for Education and Learning.

Merry, S. (2000, September). *Beyond home and school: The role of primary supports in youth development.* Chicago, IL: Chapin Hall Center for Children at the University of Chicago.

National Commission on Excellence in Education. (1983). *A nation at risk: The imperative for educational reform. A report to the nation and the Secretary of Education, United States Department of Education.* Washington, DC: Department of Education.

Rabinowitz, S., Roeber, E., Schroeder, C., & Sheinker, J. (2006). *Creating aligned standards and assessment systems* (Issue Paper No. 3). Washington, DC: Council of Chief State School Officers.

Schmoker, M., & Marzano, R. J. (1999, March). Using standards and assessments: Realizing the promise of standards-based education. *Educational Leadership, 56*(6), 17–21.

Vandell, D., & Lee, S. (1999). After-school child care programs. *The Future of Children. When School is Out, 9*(2), 64–80.

Werner, E., & Smith, R. (1982). *Vulnerable but invincible: A longitudinal study of resilient children and youth.* New York: McGraw-Hill.

1

The Science Mentoring Project[1]

How Student-to-Student Mentoring Can Encourage Motivation, Participation, and Inquiry

Cheri Fancsali

Martha was initially very hesitant to participate in afterschool Science Mentoring Project activities, especially those that involved either handling fish or taking risks such as walking out on a platform over the water to collect water samples. With encouragement from her peer mentor and other students, Martha began to participate more in such activities. Her teacher saw this increased confidence carry over into the school day in several ways. Martha became comfortable handling the classroom guinea pigs—something she was previously afraid to do—and showed more confidence in classroom discussions. She was more willing to raise her hand and offer answers or comments during classroom discussions.

[1] This chapter is based on a study of the Science Mentoring Project funded by the Robert Bowne Foundation and the National Science Foundation. Cheri Fancsali, Nancy Nevarez, Eliana Orellana, and Preeti Upadya conducted the research. The author is grateful to the teacher, students, and mentors who provided data for the study.

Martha's experience at the Science Mentoring Project fits what we know about the importance of a learning environment that encourages expression of ideas, risk taking, and questioning (National Research Council, 2005) and provides an example of how high-quality afterschool projects can have an impact on students' in-school performance. This chapter describes the Science Mentoring Project, an afterschool program with a peer-mentoring component for elementary-aged students. The chapter explains the theory supporting the design of the project, how the project operated, and how enhancing youth development competencies through the project affected participants' school performance. And it provides some lessons learned that might benefit other afterschool practitioners.

THEORETICAL FRAMEWORK

The Science Mentoring Project was guided by research on effective strategies for teaching science and fostering interest and persistence in STEM (science, technology, engineering, and mathematics) coursework and careers. As well, it was guided by studies that demonstrate that engaging, high interest afterschool activities foster students' intrinsic motivation (Vandell et al., 2005). The development of the Science Mentoring Project design was also guided by the research that points to several practices that have a positive impact on students' continuation in quantitative disciplines and science. These practices include collaborative learning and hands-on experiences. In addition, the design of the project was informed by an emphasis on practical applications and on the teaching of science in a more holistic and social context (Campbell Jolly, Hoey, & Perlman, 2002; Wenglinsky, 2000). These principles informed the design of our project, a hands-on urban ecology afterschool project using the rich resources of the Hudson River.

PROGRAM CONTEXT AND DESIGN

The Science Mentoring Project was a unique collaboration among several institutions including Educational Equity Concepts (EEC), the New York City River Project (an environmental advocacy and educational agency), and the afterschool program at a public elementary school in New York City's Lower East Side of Manhattan. The project combines EEC's After-School Science PLUS (AS+) curriculum with the River Project's field experience.

The River Project recruited 13 high school students from three New York City public high schools to serve as mentors. Two of the high schools had a science focus, and one was a comprehensive high school. Most mentors had an interest in pursuing careers or postsecondary studies in science. A few mentors did not have science-related aspirations, but were interested in teaching and working with youth.

Mentors participated in three days of training prior to working with the students. EEC staff conducted two days of training, which focused on the AS+ science curriculum and on equity issues such as encouraging equal participation by girls and boys and avoiding stereotypes. Hudson River Project staff conducted the third day of training, which focused on the specific activities and experiments used during the project. Each high school mentor worked with two fifth graders. The mentors were paid a stipend for participating in the training and the six training sessions at the River Project.

Participation in the Science Mentoring Project was open to all fifth graders in the afterschool program who expressed an interest; teachers were also asked to recommend students. Twenty students—thirteen girls and seven boys—were recruited in October 2003. Most of the students were Latino, three were Asian/Pacific Islander, and three were African American. All of the participants lived in low-income neighborhoods in New York City; they reflected the overall demographics of their Lower East Side school. About 60 percent of the school's students in 2003–2004 were English language learners, approximately one-tenth were recent immigrants, and almost all (over 99 percent) were eligible for free lunch. Just over half the students (51 percent) at this school met the standards in English language arts, and 65 percent met the standards in mathematics (New York City Department of Education, 2003).

Staff

Staff working on the project included the afterschool teacher and one staff person at the River Project. The afterschool teacher, who was also the regular day school teacher for many of the participating fifth graders, had several years of elementary-level teaching experience. She also had prior experience teaching in afterschool programs and other settings such as museums. She participated in EEC's afterschool teacher training for the AS+ curriculum. She had taught the school's afterschool program for several years and had worked with the Science Mentoring Project for two years. The teacher facilitated all of the afterschool activities from the AS+ curriculum and attended the six sessions at the River Project.

The six River Project sessions were facilitated by a staff educator from the River Project. The educator developed and facilitated the session activities. Role models were brought in, a gender and ethnically diverse group of scientists who work in a variety of science-related careers. For example, one week, two women who were New York/New Jersey Baykeepers (citizen advocates for the preservation of the Hudson-Raritan Estuary) came to speak to the group about oysters and oyster restoration. Another week, a research scientist and professor from Pace University spoke to students about his specialty, plankton ecology.

Two staff from EEC provided training and technical assistance to the afterschool teacher to support implementation of the curriculum and to facilitate the collaboration with the River Project. The EEC staff members, Maryann Stimmer and Linda Colon, are science educators. They are coauthors of the AS+ curriculum with Merle Froschl and Barbara Sprung, also of EEC. EEC staff trained the afterschool teacher, the mentors, and the River Staff educator on the AS+ curriculum. EEC staff also conducted equity training with the mentors. During implementation, EEC staff conducted observations and provided technical assistance in the classroom, at the afterschool program, and at the River Project. Finally, EEC staff coordinated logistics of the project, such as scheduling session dates, arranging for transportation, and purchasing materials.

Program Activities

The afterschool program used the curriculum every week. Activities focus on developing higher-order thinking skills such as decision making, problem solving, and creative thinking; on introducing students to diverse role models in science; and on helping students explore science careers. The curriculum is based on *National Science Education Standards*. Each activity also includes a component called The Literacy Connection, which strengthens students' reading, writing, speaking, and listening skills. Activities cover topics such as "Oobleck: Solid or Liquid?"; "Creating a Mystery Bottle"; "Sink and Float"; or "Bubble Science."

These hands-on environmental science activities are implemented at the afterschool program based at the school throughout the year, as well as at the River Project, a marine biology field station at Pier 26 in Manhattan. Students spent six two-hour sessions at the River Project working with scientists along with high school-aged mentors. Topics covered during the six sessions included water quality, oyster restoration, video microscopy, plankton ecology, and fish ecology and population. Students worked collaboratively in small groups to collect data and record observations and reflections during each session. The observations and reflections were documented in a science notebook that students kept throughout the year. For example, students collected data on water quality of the Hudson River estuary. At each visit, students recorded the air temperature, water temperature, salinity, dissolved oxygen, depth of sample, and pH. The following is an example of one student's water quality field data sheet, recorded in his science notebook.

Example of One Student's Science Notebook Entry

Date	Air Temp (°C)	Water Temp (°C)	Salinity (ppt)	Dissolved Oxygen (pbm)	Depth (m)	pH
April 16th	10°	22°	20ppt	8.6	.5m	8
April 23rd	15°	15°	16ppt	8.6	.6m	8.5
April 30th	15°	26°	13ppt	1.3	.8m	7.8
May 7th	20°	26°	40ppt	10	.4m	7.6
May 14th	19°	25°	20ppt	20	.7m	7.5

From these data, students graphed the air and water temperature and worked in small groups to make observations about the relationship between the two. Other activities included setting fish traps and inspecting and comparing fish captured by different traps. Students also performed a plankton tow to gather specimens to be documented at the station. In addition, students played games and learned songs that were related to topics such as the interdependence of the ecosystem, and they used teamwork to complete a floor-sized puzzle of the Hudson River.

The following is a description of a typical activity conducted at the River Project. This activity was designed to teach students about the characteristics of the Hudson River estuary. Estuaries are places where freshwater rivers and streams flow into the ocean, mixing with the seawater. The leader first asked students to describe the features of river (fresh) water and seawater. He then asked them to speculate about what the water would be like at an estuary where river water and salt water meet. Then, students conducted an experiment using two bottles: one was filled with fresh water and the other with seawater. The seawater was dyed with food coloring while the fresh water was not. The seawater and the fresh water were mixed and the mixture was analyzed. Students observed that the salt water settled in the bottom of the bottle while the fresh water remained on the top because salt water is heavier than fresh water.

Using the data collected at the field station, pairs of students each constructed a "report board" that included the raw data, graphs plotting change in water quality over time, oyster growth patterns, types of species in the Hudson River, and salinity of the samples in relation to the tides in the estuary. The students presented their boards to their peers and mentors at the River Project, and their boards were posted at a school fair viewed by teachers, administrators, parents, and community members.

ACADEMIC STANDARDS

Science Standards

The After-School Science PLUS (AS+) curriculum and River Project activities support the goals for school science that underlie the *National Science Education Standards*. Specifically, the goals are to educate students so that they can

- Experience the richness and excitement of knowing about and understanding the natural world;
- Use appropriate scientific processes and principles in making personal decisions;
- Engage intelligently in public discourse and debate about matters of scientific and technological concern; and
- Increase their economic productivity through the use of the knowledge, understanding, and skills of the scientifically literate person in their careers.

The standards also state that students learn science by "actively engaging in inquiries that are interesting and important to them." The standards indicate that students should "develop abilities necessary to do scientific inquiry" and "develop understanding of science as a human endeavor."

Using the scientific method to conduct experiments and explore science issues, students in this project were exposed to the nature of science, specifically, to how scientists formulate and test their explanations of nature using observation, experiments, and theoretical and mathematical models. The scientific community was also emulated by activities in small groups, where participants compared and contrasted each group's results and discussed hypotheses, observations, and interpretations.

The students, rather than mimic what real scientists do or read about what scientists do, conducted actual research in a "real-life" setting. For example, to conduct experiments at the river, students used all the science equipment and tools that scientists use, such as Vernier calipers to measure oyster growth, water quality testing materials, and Killie traps to trap fish. Students were responsible for taking care of the equipment including assembling, proper usage, as well as cleaning and disassembling equipment.

Many of the students made the connection that what they had learned in the project increased their scientific knowledge:

When we go to middle school, we will be doing chemistry. I'll be using chemicals, and I won't be afraid because I've already worked with chemicals [at the Science Mentoring Project].

If you are learning about the environment, we already know how to care for the water, and to not pollute.

The teacher also saw an increase in the students' vocabulary: "Students used words they learned at the Science Mentoring Project in class." Similarly, a student said about the project: "If you are learning about the ocean, you can use the language you've learned at the Science Mentoring Project, like brackish water, salt water, fresh water." The teacher concluded that the Science Mentoring Project helped students learn skills that would help them become better students, such as thinking and solving problems, as well as utilizing effective learning strategies.

The AS+ curriculum and the Science Mentoring Project also support several specific teaching standards including these:

- Teachers of science plan an inquiry-based science program for their students.
- Teachers structure the time available so that students are able to engage in extended investigations.
- Teachers make the available science tools, materials, media, and technological resources accessible to students.

The standards also state that teachers of science guide and facilitate learning. Specifically, teachers

Focus and support inquiries while interacting with students

Orchestrate discourse among students about scientific ideas

Challenge students to accept and share responsibility for their own learning

Recognize and respond to student diversity, and encourage all students to participate fully in science learning

Encourage and model the skills of scientific inquiry, as well as the curiosity, openness to new ideas and data, and skepticism that characterize science

The AS+ and River Project activities require teachers and facilitators to include each of these characteristics in their practice. The intense group work and collaboration that is encouraged among students, as well as the exposure to a range of other adults, both experts in the field and older youth who serve as mentors, support these teaching standards.

YOUTH DEVELOPMENT

Competencies

Through the hands-on afterschool activities, the site-based research activities, the emphasis on collaborative group work, and the mentoring component, the Science Mentoring Project aimed to develop specific positive youth development competencies in several areas.

Social Competency

The Science Mentoring Project activities fostered cooperation and group work among participants. For example, activities required students to collaborate to conduct tests and create graphs of water-quality levels and to play games with each other aimed at teaching them the interdependence of the ecological system and the importance of each person in a community. One game, called the "food chain game," involved students selecting a picture of a sea animal and then forming a big circle. The object of the game was to connect creatures at different levels of the food chain by means of a rope. After everyone was connected, the rope formed one big interconnecting web. The students representing creatures directly dependent on oysters were asked to drop the rope. Doing so caused the entire web to fall apart, showing the importance of every animal in the sea in maintaining the ecosystem.

The Science Mentoring Project activities also fostered social competency by emphasizing respect for others and for diversity. Group activities emphasized mutual respect, speaking in turn, and listening to what others had to say. In addition, the mentors and project leaders encouraged students to appreciate each other's opinions, observations, and impressions. One mentor reported that he noticed a change in his mentee's ability to work with other students. The mentor reported that, at the beginning of the project, the student tended to do "most of the work by himself" during the group activities and did not interact much with the students in his small group. At the project's end, the mentor noted that the student had "learned to let others help out with the activities."

Cognitive Competency

The students in the Science Mentoring Project had many opportunities to develop critical higher-order thinking skills as well as to add to their knowledge about environmental sciences. For example, students analyzed the reasons oysters were disappearing from the Hudson River, and they hypothesized that the oysters were disappearing because of pollution and overharvesting. Students were encouraged to use critical thinking skills by making predictions and drawing conclusions about data they collected. For example, during one of the last sessions, students created a graph of the air and water temperature data they had collected over the previous weeks. They then analyzed the relationship between the two, discovering that they were not directly proportional.

Participants learned a great deal about environmental sciences, as is evident from the following student responses to a question that asked what they learned from the Science Mentoring Project:

I learned how to use the water kit. I compared the pH levels and then did the graphs.

I learned to get the water's temperature. I learned all the equipment you need to do it.

I learned that oysters have their own language.

I learned how to observe and how to compare how things look.

At the end of the project, students reported that they knew more about environmental issues such as pollution and water quality than before the project.

Creative Competencies

Participants in the Science Mentoring Project were consistently prompted to think, make connections and observations, and ask questions—thus fostering students' creativity and communication skills. Students discussed topics with their peers and made a presentation to the group on the results of their water-quality tests at the end of the project. Writing skills were fostered by encouraging students to record observations, activities, and data in their journals.

Students were also encouraged to explore the water station and river environment using all of their senses. For one activity, students constructed a chart of what they observed by seeing, hearing, touching, and smelling. One student's response is below:

Smell	Hear
Salt	Water falling
Water	
Touch	**See**
Water	Dirty water
Cold air	Dead fish

In addition, students were encouraged to write creatively about their experiences at the river. In one activity, students were given half an hour to draw, write a poem, or write prose about their experience. These writing experiences had an impact on students, as their teacher reports: "The project gave students a place to practice speaking, volunteering answers, and writing about it. Kids need a reason and context for writing, and the project gave that to them."

Civic Competencies

The project raised students' environmental awareness and, as a result, students began to understand the importance of caring and advocating for the environment. For example, in one session students discussed environmental cleanups; the meaning of "reuse, recycle, and reduce"; and endangered fish. Students showed their increased awareness of environmental issues in their journal reflections, such as in the following entry:

> The river keepers protect the river by making sure people and factories do not dump sewage and junk in the river.

Participation in the project not only raised students' awareness of environmental concerns but also spurred their sense of responsibility for the environment. The students used what they learned to write a speech to convince other classes in the school that recycling was important. As the teacher explained, "The Science Mentoring Project helped students understand pollution and made it real to them. The students also used what they learned at the project to write a speech to convince other classes in the school that recycling was important. They started the battery recycling project at school as a result."

A Vision for the Future

The program helped students develop a vision for the future by recruiting mentors and guest speakers in scientific fields who were similar to them in terms of their racial and ethnic background, gender, and socioeconomic status. As a result, students "saw themselves" in these role models and began considering careers in the sciences. Once students saw that scientists "come in all shapes and sizes," some began talking about taking up scientific careers. For example, one student started talking about becoming a veterinarian and another talked about wanting to be a psychiatrist—careers the teacher had never heard students consider before the project.

OTHER BENEFITS AND COMPETENCIES

Engagement in School

Participation in the afterschool school program had an impact on students' school experiences in several areas; for example, students gained confidence in their abilities, increased their involvement and engagement in school, and took more responsibility for their learning. The high school mentors also had a positive impact on students, serving as models of older youth engaged in science learning, providing a caring relationship to younger students, and enhancing students' motivation in school.

According to their classroom teacher, the Science Mentoring Project helped students become more engaged with school. She reported that

> The students started getting more serious and focused in their schoolwork. At the Science Mentoring Project, they worked hard and they felt good about it. They saw the tie between what they were doing at the river and what they did at school. As a result, they worked harder in school.

One reason that this may have occurred is that the Science Mentoring Project gave students responsibility for their work and for the equipment they needed to accomplish that work. For example, students were responsible for taking careful notes on all the water-quality tests and for charting the results. They were also responsible for handling the equipment they used in experiments and for cleaning and storing the equipment properly.

Meaningful, Hands-On Activities

Activities in the program were not activities for their own sake but rather had a real-world application. For example, students in a battery recycling project collected old batteries from friends and families and arranged to have them picked up by the local battery recycling facility. This hands-on application was powerful because it gave the students a sense that they were doing something important—the activities had a purpose. The activities also fostered meaningful participation because students were conducting real experiments. Meaningful participation, assuming responsibility for carrying out tasks, completing experiments, and documenting results transformed students into active learners.

When asked to describe their favorite activity in the Science Mentoring Project, students pointed overwhelmingly to hands-on activities such as doing experiments and observing marine life firsthand.

> I like doing the experiments. In school, we just learn about these things; we don't experiment. In the Science Mentoring Project we checked the water temperature.

> It was cool to test the water and the temperature.

> Touching the oysters was my favorite part.

> Going out to the dock and pulling the net for the plankton—that was my favorite part.

According to the teacher, the enthusiasm generated through hands-on and engaging activities carried over into the classroom, motivating students to learn and helping them to assume ownership of and take responsibility for their learning. The teacher also reported that students began to ask more questions in class.

Positive Behavior

The teacher and mentors saw changes in students' behavior, motivation, and level of participation, indicating increased levels of confidence and of positive risk taking. For example, the teacher reported greater participation in activities by the girls over the course of the project. At the beginning of the project, the girls tended to "hang back" during experiments, letting the boys do all the hands-on work. Encouraged by project staff and the mentors, the girls began to take a much more active role, asserting themselves in group projects and contributing more to discussions.

For example, peer mentors wrote the following about their female mentees:

> She hesitated at first to participate, but, towards the end, she was really eager to work hands-on. She gained confidence trying new things, like touching animals and going out on the floating dock.

> She started asking more questions and became more involved in the activities. She was more willing to speak.

Both the teacher and the mentors observed that Science Mentoring Project activities helped bolster students' confidence in their ability to ask questions and to experience learning in new and different ways.

Positive Relationships With Peer Mentors

A key catalyst of the impact of the Science Mentoring Project was the mentor-mentee relationship. Students were clearly impressed by their mentors. For example, a good part of students' journal writing revolved around the mentor-mentee relationship.

> What I will remember the most is my mentor because he helped me out a lot, and he taught me a lot of stuff. He taught me about the different type of fish and crab.

> My mentor was funny. We had a good time. I wish we could meet again. I wish him a lucky year.

The teacher attributed many of the positive effects of the project to the mentors: "The mentors made a personal connection with students, which made the project more engaging and fun to students." The teacher noted that much of the project's impact on students' confidence and attitudes was due to this bond between the students and their mentors and to the positive role model the mentors provided.

SUMMARY

The experiences of students who participated in the Science Mentoring Project suggest that it helped develop youth competencies and had an impact on three areas of students' school experiences. First, the project helped increase students' engagement in school and motivation toward both school and science careers. Second, the project brought about enhanced confidence and positive changes in their classroom behaviors. Third, the project had an impact on students' skills and knowledge, for example, by increasing student awareness of environmental issues and vocabulary. The higher-order critical thinking skills that participants developed through the project's hands-on scientific exploration will be crucial for those students' academic success.

The Science Mentoring Project's impact on student engagement, motivation, and positive risk taking are important because these help build a critical foundation for student success. Youth competencies enhanced by this project are areas that are often not developed in typical day-school curricula. Afterschool programs such as the Science Mentoring Project provide an ideal setting to promote and facilitate positive youth development while, at the same time, offering fun activities that expose youth to areas of knowledge and possible career opportunities they may not otherwise experience.

Replication in Other Contexts

The Science Mentoring Project offers a model for replication in a wide variety of afterschool settings. Key components for successful replication include collaboration with science-rich institutions, sufficient training of and support for mentors, and a high-quality afterschool science curriculum such as the AS+ science curriculum. (See the appendix for information on this and other science curricula.) The following is a guideline for those interested in addressing science education during the out-of-school time:

1. Collaborate with science-rich and local institutions.
   For those interested in doing this type of afterschool project, the partnership with community environmental organizations, such the Hudson River Project environmental station, was key to the project's success. Specifically, the collaboration with the Hudson River Project provided expertise in science that many afterschool programs would not otherwise have and gave students access to meaningful and real-world experiences.

(Continued)

(Continued)

Partnering with local institutions connects student communities, drawing on local issues that can be particularly relevant. Types of community institutions include community-based environmental organizations, science and natural history museums, as well as state and federal parks. These institutions often have access to resources, such as curricula, as well as trained staff, who can support and work with staff and mentors of afterschool programs.

2. Provide training for mentors.

The relationship between youth and their high school mentors was an important part of the success of this program. While having peer mentors is ideal, careful thought needs to be done regarding the support peer mentors need to be successful in this role.

For this project, all mentors were required to participate in two full days of training implemented at the onset, as well as participate in ongoing support and training throughout the course of the project. This training included three areas: gender equity issues, science content, and how to be a mentor and role model.

3. Use an appropriate hands-on, inquiry-based science curriculum.

Grounding the activities and mentoring component in a science curriculum provided a critical framework for the development of participants' cognitive and civic competencies. Hands-on, inquiry-based science activities do not have to be expensive. All of the activities in the AS+ science curriculum use simple materials that are low cost or free and readily available (e.g., cooking oil, food coloring, recycled bottles, corn starch). As mentioned earlier, it is more important that the activities have a real-world application and be meaningful as well as purposeful.

4. Develop school-afterschool collaborations.

The Science Mentoring Project benefited from the fact that the in-school and afterschool teacher were the same. This helped provide coherence between the in-school science curriculum and the skills and knowledge being taught and reinforced in the afterschool program. For example, the teacher made connections between key concepts taught in the afterschool program (e.g., scientific method, water salinity) to work students had done in the classroom, and vice versa. While it is not critical that the in-school and afterschool teacher be the same, it is an advantage.

If, however, the afterschool and in-school teachers are different, the program would benefit from communication and collaboration between the two. Grouping the students by grade level facilitates this coherence between the school and afterschool curriculum by reducing the number of teachers and grade-level curricula with which the program must coordinate. Afterschool programs such as the Science Mentoring Project also benefit from being located in the school building. Close proximity facilitates communication between the two, making the logistics of meeting and sharing easier to navigate.

Developing a positive relationship with the school administrator is also important. Administrators can play a key role in supporting school-afterschool collaborations by providing teachers with time, space, and materials. Administrators can also play a key role in recruiting students to the afterschool program. For example, administrators may seek out and meet with parents of students they believe could benefit from the program to encourage their child's participation. Administrators and teachers can also benefit from the afterschool program. For example, the school staff can work with the afterschool staff to provide enrichment in specific areas of need, such as literacy development, or receive help in areas of the school's science curriculum with which students are struggling.

References

Campbell, P., Jolly, E., Hoey, L., & Perlman, L. (2002). *Upping the numbers: Using research-based decision making to increase the diversity in the quantitative disciplines*. Newton, MA: Education Development Center, Inc.

Miller, B. (2003). *Critical hours: Afterschool programs and educational success*. Quincy, MA: Nellie Mae Education Foundation.

National Research Council, Division of Behavioral and Social Sciences and Education, Committee on How People Learn. (2005). *How students learn: History, mathematics, and science in the classroom*. (M. S. Donovan & J. D. Bransford, Eds.) Washington: National Academies Press.

New York City Department of Education. (2003). *Annual school reports, 2002–2003*. Retrieved March 7, 2007, from http://schools.nyc.gov/daa/SchoolReports/2003-04_ASR.html

Vandell, D. L., Shernoff, D., Piece, K., Bold, D., Dadisman, K., & Brown, B. (2005). Activities, engagement, and emotion in after-school programs (and elsewhere). In H. B. Weiss, P. M. Little, & S. M. Bouffard (Eds.), *Participation in youth programs: Enrollment, attendance, and engagement: No. 105. New directions for youth development* (pp. 121–129). San Francisco, CA: Jossey-Bass.

Wenglinsky, H. (2000). *How teaching matters: Bringing the classroom back into discussions of teacher quality*. Princeton, NJ: Educational Testing Service.

RESOURCES

Web Sites

Consumers Guide to Afterschool Science Resources, www.sedl.org/afterschoolguide/science

Harvard Family Research Project (HFRP): The Out-of-School Time Learning and Development Project, http://www.gse.harvard.edu/hfrp/projects/afterschool/about.html

National Institute on Out-Of-School Time (NIOST), http://www.niost.org/

Promising Practices in Afterschool (PPAS), http://www.afterschool.org/

Science, Gender and Afterschool (SGA), http://www.afterschool.org/SGA

Curriculum/Programs

After-School Science PLUS (AS+)

This is an equity-based science program designed to facilitate fun, hands-on science activities, provide positive information about who does science, dispel stereotypes about girls and women in science, and create opportunities for students to see science as part of their everyday experience. The AS+ guide can be ordered through the EEC Web site at http://www.edequity.org, and more information about After-School Science PLUS is available at http://www.edequity.org/programs_science.php

Computer Clubhouse: Beyond Black Boxes (BBB)

This initiative seeks to engage girls (ages 9 to 14) in scientific and technological inquiry in a way that feels relevant and inviting to them. Using the mission, resources, and experience of both the Girl Scouts and the Computer Clubhouse, BBB has enabled inner-city girls to explore technology in ways that strengthen their interests and their intellectual, social, and emotional development. See the Web site http://www.computerclub house.org/programs/bbb/bbb.html.

Computer Science–Computing and Mentoring Project (CS-CAMP)

This two-week summer program at Rice University is designed for high school females. The purpose of the program is to prepare them so they will succeed with confidence and enthusiasm when they take computer science courses at their high school the next school year. The Web site is http://ceee.rice.edu/cs-camp/students/index.html.

Design It! Engineering in Afterschool Programs

This curriculum, developed by the Center for Science Education (CSE) in collaboration with the National Institute on Out-of-School Time (NIOST), provides extended design engineering activities that challenge children (ages seven to twelve) to build and refine working models of small machines and toys over a period of three to six weeks. For more information, see the Web site http://cse.edc.org/curriculum/designit/# NIOSTmanual.

Eyes to the Future

Eyes to the Future is a multiage mentoring program that supports middle school girls as they make the transition to high school and make informed choices about the opportunities available to them in high school and beyond. Eyes to the Future uses the Web to link middle school girls with high school girls in their school districts who have stayed interested in math and science and with women who use science, math, and technology in their careers. See the Web site http://etf.terc.edu/index.html for more information.

Gaining Options: Girls Investigate Real Life (GO GIRL)

This enrichment program for seventh grade girls is offered by the University of Michigan's Institute for Research on Women and Gender and held at Wayne State University. The program is funded by a National Science Foundation grant award. It encourages girls to achieve their full academic potential in mathematics by demonstrating how interesting and useful math knowledge can be. Seventh grade girls are invited to become social science researchers for ten Saturdays. For more information, consult http://www.gogirls.wayne.edu/.

Girls at the Center: Girls and Adults Learning Science Together

This curriculum developed from a national collaboration between The Franklin Institute and Girl Scouts of the USA to encourage family involvement in girls' science learning. The GAC program is designed to be effective in multiple settings, including afterschool programs. For more information, see http://www.fi.edu/tfi/programs/gac.html.

Girls Creating Games

Girls Creating Games is an afterschool program for middle school girls developed by Education, Training Research Associates (ETR). The participants are girls in Grades six to eight. The purpose of this program is to increase girls' interest, confidence, and competence in Information Technology (IT) and to encourage them to pursue educational and career paths that would keep them in the "technology pipeline." The Web site address is http://www.youthlearn.org/afterschool/GirlsCreatingGames .htm.

Girls Get SET for Life: Science, Engineering, and Technology

This program is sponsored by The Discovery Museums in Acton, MA and Tufts University School of Engineering (Medford, MA) under a grant from Lucent Technologies Foundation. The goal of the project is to promote interest and aptitude in science, engineering, and technology in teams of middle school girls by developing and producing museum exhibits to be displayed in The Science Discovery Museum. Consult http://engineering.tufts.edu/ggs/ for more information.

Girls in Science (University of Kentucky)

This program aims to encourage middle school girls to pursue careers in science, technology, engineering, and math. Beginning in the summer, rising seventh grade girls participate in this two-year program. The Girls in Science program includes a one-week summer camp at the University of Kentucky, Saturday Academies throughout the school year, and mentoring relationships. For more information, see http://www.mc.uky.edu/behavioralscience/girlsinscience.asp

Girls Reaching Out With Science (GROWS)

A program that brings together undergraduate female science and education majors with middle school girls in order to support girls pursuing science in the form of a science fair project. Consult the program's Web site at http://capital2.capital.edu/orgs/GROWS/.

Operation SMART (Science Math and Relevant Technology)

Girls Incorporated launched Operation SMART in 1985. In hundreds of sites across the country, close to a quarter of a million girls between the ages of six and eighteen have started on the path to becoming engineers, auto mechanics, microsurgeons, and astronauts. They're asking questions, making guesses, taking chances. See http://www.girlsinc.org/ic/page.php?id=1.2.1.

PDK Poster Project: Using Visual Means to Challenge Stereotypes

The PDK Project has two major goals: to promote "awareness and appreciation of science and technology by humanizing the image of research science and scientists" and to support women and girls who choose to pursue careers related to the physical sciences and mathematics. The site's resources include thirty-six visually stunning posters; study guides to accompany each poster; videos, interviews, and biographies of the poster participants; links to related sites; and more. See http://www.pdksciart.com/poster27.htm.

SciGirls—Free Hands-on Girl-Focused Science Inquiry Materials

DragonflyTV's SciGirls is a collaborative program funded by the National Science Foundation that empowers PBS outreach professionals to partner with local youth organizations, educators, and parents to deliver hands-on science encouragement and career guidance to girls in their communities. It is based on DragonflyTV, a half-hour, weekly television program showcasing eager young scientists, ages nine to twelve, engaged in authentic science inquiry. SciGirls activity guides are available for download on the PBS Web site: http://pbskids.org/dragonflytv/parentsteachers/scigirls .html.

Other Resources

National Science Education Standards is available for sale from the National Academy Press, Box 285, 2101 Constitution Avenue, N.W., Washington, D.C. 20055. http://newton.nap.edu/html/nses/

The Academy for Educational Development (AED)

Founded in 1961, AED is an independent, nonprofit organization committed to solving critical social problems and building the capacity of individuals, communities, and institutions to become more self-sufficient. AED works in all the major areas of human development, with a focus on improving education, health, and economic opportunities for the least advantaged in the United States and developing countries throughout the world. The AED Center for School and Community Services uses multidisciplinary approaches to address critical issues in education, health, and youth development. Its work is informed by the core values of equity, excellence, collaboration, and democratic participation. And the organization is guided by a vision of families, youth, community members, and professionals working in partnership to develop and promote effective programs and services. For more information on AED, see http://www.aed.org/.

The Educational Equity Center (EEC) at AED

The mission of the Educational Equity Center is to provide equality of opportunity on a national scale in schools and afterschool settings, starting in early childhood. The Center is an outgrowth of Educational Equity Concepts, a national nonprofit organization with a twenty-two-year history of addressing educational excellence for all children regardless of gender, race/ethnicity, disability, or level of family income. EEC's goal is to ensure that equity is a key focus within national reform efforts, eliminating inequities that often limit student potential.

The River Project

The River Project is a marine science field station based at Pier 26, on the lower west side of Manhattan, in New York City. Founded in 1986, The River Project works to protect and restore the Hudson River ecosystem through scientific research, hands-on environmental education, and urban habitat improvement. For more information on The River Project, go to http://www.riverproject.org.

2

In Addition Afterschool Mathematics Program

Helping Students Learn to Think Critically

Judith McVarish

The children and I had spent the previous day making observations in two different parks. Their notebooks showed lists of questions they had written about the people, the playground equipment, and the space. I began getting the children prepared for their next project.

Tricia: Does anyone want to talk a bit about something that they observed yesterday?

Jamila: I was looking at the people that were there, and I thought that there were more people at the first park that we went to.

Kira: That's because it's better.

Taylor: And it's bigger and has sand.

Tricia: Did anyone count the number of people at each park?

Oscar: Yes, there were twenty-eight people at Kelly Park (first park) and thirteen at Seal Park (second park).

Kelissa:	I don't think that that means that more people always go to Kelly Park. It could just be that there are more kids in that area.
Jamila:	Or that there are more babies, because I think Kelly Park is a baby park.
Tricia:	What could we do to answer this question of whether one park always has more people than the other park?
Rasheed:	We could go and count them and write it down.
Reed:	But we need to go more than once if we want to say if it always happens.
Tricia:	What do you mean?
Reed:	Well, we would have to go like three times to make sure that Kelly Park always has more people.
Kelissa:	I was also wondering what most people who go to the park do while they are there.

SOURCE: Instructor's field notes.

The reform movement in mathematics education (National Council of Teachers of Mathematics, 1991, 2000; National Research Council, 1989) provides a clear vision of mathematical learning. This includes creating learning opportunities that engage students so that they feel confident in their ability to solve mathematical problems as well as recognize mathematics as relevant in their everyday lives. The literature recommends building mathematical communities where students present, question, and defend their ideas and thinking, with an emphasis on logic, problem solving, and reasoning over memorization, procedural thinking, and right answers.

The In Addition afterschool project reenvisions math. We seek to engage children in learning mathematics by encouraging students to ask their own questions and seek answers to those questions. This chapter describes the project's founding principles and how we work to shape our daily practice around inquiry-based math learning during the out-of-school time and in the context of the urban community. We will also describe the basis of the program in youth development and how it is firmly aligned with learning standards. Finally, we describe the real-life challenges and pitfalls of implementing this type of program, as well as some strategies that have worked to address these challenges.

THEORETICAL FRAMEWORK

The National Council of Teachers of Mathematics (NCTM, 2000) posits that mathematical understanding increases when students are engaged in real-life, problem-based learning. The National Research Council (NRC, 2001) recommends providing students with opportunities to investigate ideas collaboratively as a community of learners in order to discover multiple strategies that lead to a deeper understanding of mathematics. Collaborative questioning and conversation can also contribute to a sense of shared learning that reduces the competitive inclinations often associated with a traditional learning environment. Steven Levy, the author of *Starting from Scratch* (1996), suggests, "Asking questions promotes an interest in the 'Other,' acting as a balance to the self-absorption and the self-centeredness that so pervades our culture" (Levy, 1996, p. 37).

Many elementary schools are not afforded such learning opportunities. "Surveys of U.S. teachers have consistently shown that nearly all their instructional time is structured around textbooks or other commercially produced materials, even though teachers vary substantially in the extent to which they follow a book's organization and suggested activities" (NRC, 2001, p. 36). In responding to a 1996 National Assessment of Educational Progress (NAEP) mathematics assessment, teachers reported that fourth graders were usually tested in mathematics once or twice a month. About one-third of the children took tests once or twice a week, even though more frequent testing was associated with lower achievement (NRC, 2001, p. 40). Over 90 percent of these teachers reported that they gave considerable emphasis to facts, concepts, skills, and procedures; only 52 percent focused on reasoning processes and even fewer, 30 percent, on communication.

Teachers explain the disparity between mathematics reform goals and the realities of the classroom as "not having enough time" to help students discover mathematics. Sometimes curriculum and testing pressures, fueled by an ever-increasing mantra of accountability based on standardized tests (Eisner, 2003), place rigid teaching and learning expectations on teachers and students. While rigid adherence to curriculum is meant to help students achieve higher test scores, national results show that this emphasis is not working (Eisner, 2002). The cost, however, is a loss of joy about learning mathematics that not only decreases learning potential but also produces mathematics anxiety and frequently leaves students with a view that mathematics is a discrete set of skills with no relevance to their lives. Mathematics learning then becomes rote and compliant memorization of facts and procedures in which students merely plug in a formula to get the desired answer to an isolated, irrelevant question.

Our beliefs about how children learn, powered by our experiences as mathematics educators and guided by the literature, provided the theoretical framework on which we shaped our ideas about integrating inquiry-based math learning in the afterschool time in an urban community. The result was the In Addition After School Learning Principles:

1. Children learn when they are engaged and fascinated.

Encouraging children to explore things they wonder about and to think about new questions creates a cycle of excitement. Instead of being drudgery, learning becomes an enjoyable, satisfying experience that begs to be repeated over and over again in a variety of new circumstances (Dewey, 1916).

2. Children learn when they share their ideas and thinking with others in a community of learning.

Building urban learning communities of trust (Ennis & McCauley, 2002; Wayne, 2002) leads to socially and experientially constructed learning that enhances people's ability to discuss ideas, develop reasoning capabilities, and establish a habit of collaborative problem posing and solving. A learning environment in which respect for the thinking of all is the norm allows students to think about things from new perspectives.

3. Children learn when their learning is embedded in themselves, their homes, and their communities.

Combining the recommendations of the National Research Council and the National Council of Teachers of Mathematics, as well as our own set of beliefs, the In Addition afterschool program aims to facilitate the teaching and learning of mathematics outside of classroom constraints such as high stakes testing and grades. Though basic math skills are important, these skills are developed via providing students opportunities to learn mathematics when the motivation to learn comes from within. Students' questions and interests guide learning investigations linked to their neighborhood. Students help each other become more aware of and connected to their community by examining their world through the lenses of their diverse backgrounds. Parent participation, through workshops and retreats, provides both a support system for students and links home, school, and community.

PROGRAM CONTEXT AND DESIGN

In Addition is situated in two public elementary schools in New York City. In early September of each year, flyers are distributed in each school to every student in Grades three, four, and five, inviting them to consider participation in the In Addition afterschool program. Students are randomly selected from the returned applications through a lottery system, taking five students each from the third, the fourth, and the fifth grades. We did not limit the opportunity to distinct populations such as gifted or at-risk students because we wanted to ensure a heterogeneous group. We did this because we believe that the ability to think critically is necessary, and possible, for all learners. We believe that, as a society, we cannot afford to limit access to opportunities to learn how to think and reason and ask questions to any single, elite, chosen population. The only criterion for acceptance was a commitment to attend two hours a day, three days a week, from September to May.

The In Addition project team is comprised of university professors, two New York City classroom teachers who teach the afterschool program in their own classrooms from 3–5 PM, and a research consultant who documented the project, which included gathering instructor field notes, videotapes, student focus groups, and parent interviews.

Content and Activities

A typical day in the In Addition program begins with a daily graphing question followed by discussion. For example, this sentence is posted on a magnetic board: "I would rather travel by . . . car, bike, train, airplane, boat, motorcycle, subway, bus, or other." Students place tiles with their initials on them in a category to create a graph on the board. The ensuing discussion involves issues of time, destination, budgets, companions, experience, and purpose of travel.

Students then work in small groups on ongoing projects. In Addition is designed to help students conduct their own mathematical investigations based on topics in their community, topics that interest them. To begin this process, the students and instructor went on several exploration walks around their neighborhood. They looked at parks, bridges, trees and plants, the river, and the cultures of the community. As the students observed these things, they wrote questions and noted things that they would like to investigate further. Small groups of four to five students were formed based on the topics students most wanted to study. Each group works independently during this small group time. The instructor's role is to act as a guide for the students by helping them focus their questions, provide resources, and organize field trip experiences.

The following description of the Bridge Group is an example of how an interest in a topic led to other areas of inquiry, and also offered rich mathematics learning opportunities. This particular group of students began its investigation by thinking about this question: "What kind of materials do they use to build bridges?" This led the students to wonder how bridges stayed up. They walked across one of the neighborhood bridges noticing the structure, materials, distance, and height. Students built a model of a bridge out of paper and masking tape that could hold five pounds. Different types of structural properties were examined and discussed. This investigation gave new direction to the students' inquiry, and we found them asking questions such as, "Are all bridges built the same way?" A natural outcome of these wonderings was a comparison of other bridges in the city, with students noting different structural patterns and bridge lengths.

As students went on these bridge trips, they began to take an interest in the people walking on the bridges. This directed their thinking to why bridges are so important to this community. How do people use bridges?

How long does it take to cross the bridge during different times of the day or using different modes of travel? To find answers to some of these questions, they wanted to interview people walking on the bridge. They prepared questions to ask, discussed and practiced interview methods, and learned how to operate a video camera. Students then conducted interviews.

As a result of their interviews, students compiled a list of questions with which to survey their school community. Because most of the students had never actually walked across any of the New York City bridges, they were curious to find out who had in their school and neighborhood. We discussed survey methods, such as sampling, tallying, and charting. The students collected their data and used graphing software to present their findings to the rest of the class. This presentation led to a whole class discussion, involving predictions and the probability of their findings, with the Bridge Group acting as discussion leaders. After analyzing this data set, students expressed a desire to conduct a new survey with different questions and new populations.

The Bridge Group was one of four groups completing projects during one program cycle. The other projects included River and Water, People and Cultures, and Television in the Community. Each of the four groups presented aspects of its investigation project to the other groups and to the families of all group members during a spring retreat. The goal of the presentations was to involve parents and peers in a discussion about findings.

Here are examples of the other groups' investigations:

- The People and Cultures Group used the Internet to map migration patterns of people in their community from their original homelands;
- The Park Group, as illustrated in the opening vignette, studied neighborhood parks and their usage patterns;
- The Water Group analyzed survey results on student water usage; and
- The TV Group figured out how to represent their data results from previous interviews they conducted in the school about television-watching preferences.

The day closes with a large group discussion of the groups' progress, challenges, and successes, as well as with the identification of new questions emerging for investigation.

The following journal entry represents one student's learning experience:

Student Journal Entry (1/14/2003)

We had a lot of fun doing our interviews. We had five questions that we wanted to ask people on the bridges. I held the video camera, and Kayla asked the questions to the people passing by. It was hard to get them to stop, though. Some people actually ignored us when we tried talking to them. Now, that's just rude! Most of the people we did talk to were visiting, and it was their first time walking over the Brooklyn Bridge. One person said that they came all the way from Italy to see New York City. And one man said that he crosses the bridge every day to go to work. That bridge is so long and it was so cold out there, I would never want to cross it every day.

It was extremely important that the instructor be well grounded in our educational philosophy and approach to math activities but also skilled in building a community of trust. Choosing the New York City classroom teachers who would serve as the afterschool instructors was beneficial because they a) provided an understanding of school culture and academic expectations and b) encouraged mathematics investigations involving active dialogue and debate. The instructor needed to understand classroom management—to create a learning environment in which children feel comfortable challenging each other and accepting divergent points of view. Over time, we envisioned, the teachers would bring back what they were learning about mathematics instruction in the In Addition project to their own school classrooms.

ACADEMIC STANDARDS

The majority of the fifty states derive their mathematics learning standards from the National Teachers of Mathematics (NCTM) Standards. The following content standards from the *Principles and Standards for School Mathematics* (NCTM, 2000) are consistently addressed in the In Addition program:

Algebra
Understand patterns, relations, and functions

Use mathematical models to represent and understand quantitative relationships

Analyze change in various contexts

Measurement
Apply appropriate techniques, tools, and formulas to determine measurements

Data Analysis and Probability
Formulate questions that can be addressed with data, and collect, organize, and display relevant data to answer them

Select and use appropriate statistical methods to analyze data

Develop and evaluate inferences and predictions that are based on data

Understand and apply basic concepts of probability

The activities of both the Bridge Group and Park Group are examples of students engaged in meaningful learning relative to this standard. Students in both groups formulated their questions, collected data, and analyzed their data. They also made inferences and predictions based on their data analysis. The following chart analyzes how the Bridge Group project activities were aligned with the following mathematics concepts and standards from the National Council of Teachers of Mathematics (2000).

Table 1   Principles and Standards for Mathematics Explored in Bridge Project

Geometry	Analyze characteristics and properties of two and three dimensional geometric shapes, and develop mathematical arguments about geometric relationships
Measurement	Apply appropriate techniques, tools, and formulas to determine measurements
Representation	Use representations to model and interpret physical, social, and mathematical phenomena
Data Analysis and Probability	Formulate questions that can be addressed with data, and collect, organize, and display relevant data to answer them
	Select and use appropriate statistical methods to analyze data
	Develop and evaluate inferences and predictions that are based on data
	Understand and apply basic concepts of probability
Problem Solving	Apply and adapt a variety of appropriate strategies to solve problems
	Solve problems that arise in mathematics and in other contexts
Reasoning and Proof	Select and use various types of reasoning and methods of proof
Communication	Communicate mathematical thinking coherently and clearly to peers, teachers, and others
Connections	Recognize and apply mathematics in context outside of mathematics

SOURCE: National Council of Teachers of Mathematics, 2000.

NCTM's five process standards are also addressed in the afterschool program. These include problem solving, reasoning and proof, communication, connections, and representation. These processes reflect the manner in which mathematics is learned and how students acquire and use knowledge. In Addition's curriculum is clearly rooted in the learning principles in these standards. For example, a question that arose for students at one of the schools was why kids fight at their school so often. Their subsequent study exemplifies the process standards of problem solving, reasoning and proof, communication, connections, and representation. The following report was written by the students in the afterschool program:

Report on Fighting at School

This year, we wanted to know why kids fight in our school. It is a problem for us. We don't want kids to fight because they could get injured or hurt. We did surveys and interviews in our school to help us answer our question. We interviewed three teachers, the principal, the assistant principal, and secretary. We surveyed about 125 students in Grades three to five. We thought doing surveys and interviews of these people would help us understand why kids fight.

Survey Results:

We asked about 125 students four different questions. When all of our data was collected, we tallied the responses and created graphs to show what we learned.

What we learned from the interviews:

When we interviewed the teachers about why they thought kids in our school fight, they said that students get into fights for a lot of different reasons. They are that students get frustrated when they don't get their own way, or they just want attention; they think they are tough, or they try to defend themselves. Teachers also said that students fight for no reason at all.

Teachers said they try to prevent fights in many ways. Some encourage their students to work out their problems. Other teachers separate their kids from fights. The teachers mostly try to prevent fights before they happen.

We interviewed our school secretary and found out something amazing. She said she thought that kids fight more today than in the past. We think this might be because students were physically punished for misbehaving. Today, kids don't seem to care. They know that they will have some sort of punishment, but it won't be physical.

Conclusion:

This study has shown us that fighting is a problem in our school. It's happening in classrooms and in the yard. A major reason it's happening is because kids want attention.

Students continued their interest in the "fighting dilemma" by focusing on the prevention aspect. They approached the school principal with a plan to have student playground monitors who would oversee playground games and provide an unbiased intervention in cases of game rule confusion. They requested "Playground Monitor" T-shirts from the principal and worked out a monthly monitor recess schedule. Nowhere is a sense of purpose more encouraged with youth than in activities by which they are identifying a real-life problem and finding a solution that addresses the needs of all.

YOUTH DEVELOPMENT

According to Carl Rogers (1974), significant learning occurs when students are trusted to learn knowledge that is not neatly prepackaged mathematical knowledge organized to help them learn. By adopting this learning stance for In Addition learners, we have confidence in youth's natural ability to produce learning that is of value and importance to them. Therefore, significant learning for us is helping students free their minds of "right answers" and become more interested in developing habits of independent thinking. We work to provide dynamic learning opportunities that will shape mathematics thinking beyond the classroom.

A goal of In Addition is to support learning that makes a difference in the lives of the young people. We attempt to do so by creating opportunities so that they will take responsibility for the quality of their lives and by encouraging them to pose and answer their own questions about the world in which they live. The youth development framework at the heart of the In Addition afterschool program is situated in resiliency theory. It also draws from the work of Garmezy, Masten, and Tellegen (1984) who identified outcomes of youth development including social competence, problem-solving skills, and sense of purpose that support resiliency in children.

The diagram that follows shows the cohesion between the learning orientation theory of Carl Rogers (top of diagram) and Garmezy's learning capacities (bottom of diagram) and the way in which they both contribute to building resiliency and significant learning in our In Addition afterschool learners.

Social Competency

Youth participate in and learn how to be a member of a support network composed of peers, family, teachers, and community. In Addition creates this community in a variety of ways. One important way is by spending time together on overnight retreats held twice a year. At each retreat, youth, parents, and In Addition staff eat, solve problems, participate in math learning activities, and relax as a family. The emphasis is on building social relationships and on the ways in which the environment,

Figure 2.1   Significant Learning and Resiliency

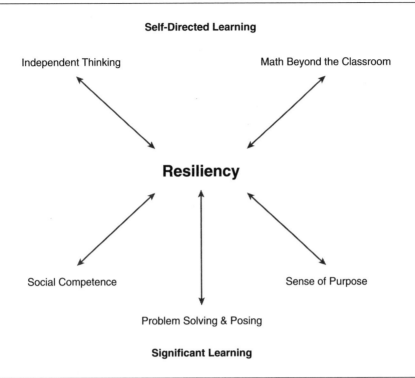

individuals, and groups interact in the process of gaining knowledge about the world.

Throughout our time together in the retreats, children reach out to other children, parents nurture children other than their own, teachers experience the joy of going on a student/parent-created treasure hunt, and parents and children make new friends from other schools. The emphasis on relationships engenders family, a social network, as well as a community to support and strengthen growth and development.

Problem Posing and Problem Solving

The expectation for participants in the afterschool program is to solve problems within our learning community—to be reflective, to question that which is not understood, and to be persistent in these investigations. This is done, on a consistent basis, through the math instruction during the afterschool program. However, students also engage in posing problems and solving critical issues in their schools and community. As mentioned, one project group researched why kids were fighting at school, and members conducted surveys and interviews with teachers, school secretaries, and students.

Sense of Purpose

The real-life aspect of all our activities, and their connection to communities, provides a sense of purpose for our students. They are using math both to explore their communities and to address key issues in a purposeful manner. In this setting, math is not set apart as a purely academic subject. Rather, students are shown that math can be connected to pragmatic uses and can aid in young people's sense of efficacy and in their ability to make an impact on their environment.

OTHER BENEFITS AND COMPETENCIES

Parent Involvement

Parents became our most valuable support system. We noticed that each year parent involvement increased. Parents began to trust our efforts to help their children to learn mathematics in novel ways. We held meetings every other month with a group of parents from each school. During these meetings, parents came up with new ideas, analyzed their children's journal writing, and shared in the mathematical thinking and research that was taking place.

In addition, parents participated in our retreats, expressing their delight in being able to participate in as well as observe their children learning to look at the world through a mathematical lens. They were able to take part in math learning activities such as measuring the circumference of trees, measuring the depth of the water, and creating kites that would fly. Eventually, parents became advocates of math education that was different than their own, often problematic, math experiences at school. Also, parents became articulate about how they wanted their children educated, and they initiated a discussion with the principal of their children's school. They asked that math teaching be more than test preparation sessions.

Negotiating the Tests

We intentionally designed In Addition to help children learn in a test-free context. What we did not expect was the way school-based testing hovered like a dark cloud over our learning community. The forces in education and city politics that emphasize accountability in the form of "passing the test" made it impossible to escape the power of testing over the learning process. During the first year, we began to counter the negative influence of the tests by incorporating discussions in our bimonthly parent workshops. We talked about how to reduce the stress of testing, offered test-taking strategies, and raised awareness of the impact of high-stakes testing. During our second year, we continued to work to ameliorate the test syndrome without destroying children's and parents' faith in their school.

November of our third year, when testing mania almost closed down our project, we decided to attack the problem with a more creative solution. On any given day of the afterschool sessions, only four or five children were in attendance due to a conflicting school test preparation program. Students identified as "at-risk" were recommended for the test prep classes. Parents were conflicted. They wanted their children to continue with the In Addition program, but they wanted to ensure their children were not hurt by the consequences of the high-stakes testing. The school had set up test preparation sessions after school, assigning students to particular days, times, and subjects for their tutoring. Ironically, one parent told us her child would not be returning to In Addition until April because the principal told her that her child needed *math* tutoring.

The In Addition team met with parents and the principals from each school and suggested a "Parents as Teachers" option. After meeting with the two principals involved and spending time locating test prep materials for parents, we called an emergency meeting for all parents of In Addition children. The principals attended as well as most of the In Addition parents. We clearly presented the dilemma facing the program. Children could not continue in the In Addition afterschool program if their attendance was going to be sporadic or if they were able to come only one day a week because they needed to attend test prep meetings after school. If parents wanted their children to continue in our program, we were offering them an alternative. In Addition would provide parents with test prep materials and teach them how to teach their children at home on weekends or evenings. We did not downplay the seriousness of this choice. It would mean a huge commitment on the part of the parents. Parents expressed concerns; they worried about not knowing enough math, about the limited available time they had to commit to such a task, and about the possibility that their children would not pass the test if they were the test prep teachers. We conveyed our commitment to making this work and set up monthly workshops for parents to learn the math to help them tutor their children. Every parent in the program agreed to participate and take on this test prep tutoring responsibility.

The parent's dedication to helping their children learn this material was amazing. As the test date approached, we gathered both afterschool groups together for an evening of test prep strategies and pizza. Children and parents worked as teams to learn ways to take the test and to get ready for the day of the test. Both parents and students exhibited confidence about the pending test. After five months of parents doing test prep and students NOT attending the school test prep sessions, every single In Addition student passed the standardized test: a meaningful result with major implications.

Negotiating Homework

We did not include homework help in our project design, nor did we assign homework. From the very first day, In Addition students wanted to know why they couldn't do their homework. We were not surprised to find that the children's math homework consisted of computational, one-answer, short-response workbook problems. Spelling homework often involved writing words three times each and putting the words into sentences. Reading and social studies homework consisted of comprehension questions.

One day our daily graphing question asked, "How much time do you spend doing homework a night?" A majority of students answered that they spent an hour to an hour and a half on homework each night.

Two students dropped out of In Addition during the first year because the pressure of homework was too great. The reality was that students left the program at 5 PM facing an hour or two of homework before bedtime. By November of that first year, we decided that we had to respect the students' and parents' needs to have some homework completed during this afterschool time, so the evening at home would be less stressful. After discussion with the children, we came to a compromise that extended the afterschool program for thirty minutes to allow time for homework. We spoke with the principal and assistant principal about the homework issue and explained our solution.

This compromise, however, was a short-term answer. Our ultimate goal is to engage teachers and administrators in discussions about how much homework and what kind of homework is necessary. We spoke with the assistant principal at one school about setting a meeting to discuss the possibility of changing the school's homework policy for the following year. His response was neutral, and our plan is to continue to pursue this goal. At this juncture, our strategy is working: The children seem less harried and attendance is not suffering, yet the homework problem still persists.

SUMMARY

We continue to learn each day in our work with this project, yet we are aware we don't know enough. What we have shared is our beginning, not an end point. Children are being shown how to learn to think and reason abstractly by posing problems and finding mathematical solutions to issues that are of interest to them. In the search for understanding, we expect and hope that they discover the need for persistence as each question leads them to new questions.

The In Addition story continues to unfold and to have an impact on its leaders, the students, their parents, and their classroom teachers. Rome wasn't built in a day, and school change doesn't happen as rapidly as we would like. As John Dewey (1916) notes, "Growing is not something which is completed in odd moments; it is a continuous leading into the future" (p. 65). As we begin each new year, we continued to grapple with the challenges. Our strategy depends on keeping our vision intact and remaining true to what we believe are practices that promote significant learning for our students.

Replication in Other Contexts

For anyone thinking about establishing an afterschool program similar to the one described here, I offer a few words of advice. First, keep the community in the foreground. Whether you live in an urban context, a suburb, or you are wishing to situate the afterschool program in a rural setting—the resources of the community provide the fodder for mathematical projects. This is true mainly because the community is where the students live and therefore has vast possibilities for questions and the means to connect math learning in real ways to their lives.

The second piece of advice is to be clear about what matters and what does not. If the goal is to help children learn mathematics with engagement, then it is imperative to suspend the urge to test or to prepare students for taking tests.

Third, listen to what the children want to know and are interested in finding more about. This becomes the curriculum. It is your responsibility to guide the process and offer possible resources in order to deepen the learning experience.

Here are 10 "musts" to consider when establishing a similar program.

1. *The instructors are key.* Interview candidates to determine if their educational philosophy is aligned with the inquiry-based goals and philosophy of the program. Sometimes local colleges of education have preservice teachers or graduate students who are being trained in this approach and need to be placed in an instructional setting for field service hours.

2. *Take the first few weeks or the first month to develop a sense of community with one another.* Children need to feel safe in order to share their thinking publicly.

3. *Meet together as a staff on a regular basis.* This provides support and validation that what you are doing is worthwhile. Our meetings always involved food, a pot luck meal twice a month during which we planned what to do, shared ideas, and offered support in a variety of ways.

4. *Utilize the community.* Depending on what the children are interested in knowing, locate people, services, city departments, and other organizations that might provide resources for their investigations.

5. *Parents are the greatest assets—include them from day one.* They were our biggest allies and provided assistance, support, and a sense of humor.

6. *Be patient with yourself.* It takes time to see results. Students do not initially trust that you honestly want them to ask their own questions rather than seek the "correct" answer.

(Continued)

(Continued)

> 7. *As much trouble and expense as the weekend retreats may appear to be, they are essential.* We began with only one retreat, at the close of the year, and decided that it was such a bonding experience that we needed to begin the year with a retreat as well.
>
> 8. *Find ways to build relationships with the school.* Offer to run workshops for teachers on inquiry-based mathematics learning, invite teachers to observe any time, and send the principal and assistant principal an invitation to the weekend retreats.
>
> 9. *Discuss homework policies up front with students, parents, and administrators.* Work out a plan for how to handle this issue that respects all constituents.
>
> 10. *Last, enjoy the experience.* If you are engaged there is a greater likelihood your students will be excited about learning.

References

Dewey, J. (1916). *Democracy and education: An introduction to the philosophy of education.* New York: Macmillan.

Eisner, E. (2002). The kind of schools we need. *Phi Delta Kappan, 83*(8), 576–583.

Eisner, E. (2003). Questionable assumptions about schooling. *Phi Delta Kappan, 84*(9), 648–657.

Ennis, C., & McCauley, T. (2002). Creating urban communities worthy of trust. *Journal of Curriculum Studies, 34*(2), 149–172.

Garmezy, N., Masten, A. S., & Tellegen, A. (1984). The study of stress and competence in children: A building block for developmental psychology. *Child Development, 55*, 97–111.

Kohn, A. (2000). *The case against standardized testing: Raising the scores, ruining the schools.* Portsmouth, NH: Heinemann.

Levy, S. (1996). *Starting from scratch: One classroom builds its own curriculum.* Portsmouth, NH: Heinemann.

McLaughlin, M. (2000). Community counts. *Educational Leadership, 58*(7), 14–18.

National Council of Teachers of Mathematics. (1991). *Professional standards for teaching mathematics.* Reston, VA: Author.

National Council of Teachers of Mathematics. (2000). *Principles and standards for school mathematics.* Reston, VA: Author.

National Institute on Out-of-School Time. (2000). *Making an impact on out-of-school time.* Wellesley, MA: Wellesley College.

National Research Council. (1989). *Everybody counts: A report to the nation on the future of mathematics education.* Washington, DC: National Academy Press.

National Research Council. (2001). *Adding it up: Helping children learn mathematics.* Washington, DC: National Academy Press.

Rogers, C. (1974). Significant learning: In therapy and in education. In R. T. Hyman (Ed.), *Teaching: Vantage points for study* (pp. 269–282). Philadelphia: J. B. Lippincott Company.

Wayne, M. (2002). Getting smarter. In D. Worsley (Ed.), *Teaching for depth: Where math meets the humanities* (pp. 124–134). Portsmouth, NH: Heinemann.

RESOURCES

Burns, M. (1982). *Math for smarty pants.* Boston: Little, Brown and Company.

Carnegie Council on Adolescent Development. (1992). *A matter of time: Risk and opportunity in the non-school hours—Report of the Task Force on Youth Development and Community Programs.* New York: Carnegie Corporation of New York.

Davis, R. B. (1986). Conceptual and procedural knowledge in mathematics: A summary analysis. In J. Hiebert (Ed.), *Conceptual and procedural knowledge: The case of mathematics* (pp. 260–278). Hillside, NJ: Lawrence Erlbaum Associated.

Johmann, C., & Rieth, E. (1999). *Bridges: Amazing structures to design, build and test.* Charlotte, VT: Williamson Publishing Company.

Levy, S. (1996). *Starting from scratch: One classroom builds its own curriculum.* Portsmouth, NH: Heinemann.

Mokros, J. (1996). *Beyond facts and flashcards: Exploring math with your kids.* Portsmouth, NH: Heinemann.

Parker, R. (1993). *Mathematical power: Lessons from a classroom.* Portsmouth, NH: Heinemann.

Rowan, T., & Bourne, B. (1994). *Thinking like mathematicians.* Portsmouth, NH: Heinemann.

Schoenfeld, A. H. (1992). Learning to think mathematically: Problem solving, meta-cognition, and sense making in mathematics. In D. A. Grouws (Ed.), *Handbook of research on teaching and learning* (pp. 334–370). Old Tappan, NJ: Macmillan.

Smith, D. (2002). *If the world were a village: A book about the world's people.* Toronto, ON: Kids Press, Ltd.

Stenmark, J., Thompson, V., & Cossey, R. (1986). *Family math.* Berkeley, CA: Lawrence Hall of Science.

Sturges, P. (1998). *Bridges are to cross.* New York: Putnam Press.

UNESCO. (n.d.). *Education.* Retrieved March 9, 2007, from http://www.unesco.org/education/

Vandell, D., & Posner, J. (1999). After-school activities and the development of low-income urban children: A longitudinal study. *Developmental Psychology, 35*(3), 868–879.

3

Civic Connections

Practicing Democracy Through Debate Clubs in the Out-of-School Time Hours

Georgia Hall

It's a crisp Saturday morning in March in the Bronx, and about 200 youth are packing into Wing's Academy school cafeteria for one of many New York Urban Debate Tournaments. They are wearing usual teen attire: low-slung jeans, baseball caps, and knapsacks. It is only 8:00 in the morning. There are cell phone conversations, and the soda machine is active. But there are also round tables with groups of youth holding portfolios, tapping laptop keys, and shuffling manila envelopes labeled "Negative" and "Affirmative." A middle school–aged girl is practicing dialog while her peer listens. The peer offers some advice: "You should add more emotion to your last paragraph." She tries again. More convinced, her friend approves.

Immense pressure on school systems to meet academic and testing benchmarks has contributed to radical changes in school schedules, course offerings, and scholastic expectations. Many traditional components such as civics education have gradually been taken out of the school day.[1]

---

[1] While political science literature may distinguish between the terms *democracy, citizenship, civic education*, and *civic engagement*, for the purposes of this chapter, the author uses them interchangeably.

Opportunities for civics education have not only diminished in traditional learning settings but also are inequitably distributed. Young people who do not have regular discussion about politics are more likely to be African Americans or Hispanics, not college bound, and not Internet users, who have less education than others their age and are not registered to vote (Soule, 2001). In turn, lack of civic engagement contributes to existing educational, economic, and employment inequities.

Civic education, or what we are calling *democracy skill-building experiences*, can help to empower youth to become engaged learners, critical thinkers, and active citizens, as well as to be more academically prepared. At a time when the civic participation of young people is becoming less frequent, out-of-school time and youth development programs, such as an urban debate club, offer a possible model for using the out-of-school time hours to foster civic participation, democracy skill building, and learning.

This chapter describes an urban youth debate league and how this type of program can be a part of the vision of a more informed and active youth citizenry. This chapter discusses these questions: What might "democracy in action" look like in out-of-school time and youth development programs, and how does it relate to learning? How does urban debate serve as an example of democracy skill building during the out-of-school time hours? What are the program and policy supports needed to support a civic engagement and democracy skill-building role for out-of-school time and youth development programs? The chapter concludes with information important for youth program providers, policy makers, and other individuals and organizations seeking to foster youth democracy development and participation during the out-of-school time hours.

THEORETICAL FRAMEWORK

Democracy and Civic Engagement

There is consensus that to preserve a democracy requires the development of democratic citizens. How we think about the formation of democratic citizens depends on the specific conception of democracy we hold, whether it is a set of skills, level of participation, civic discourse, community mobilization, or exercise of certain rights and responsibilities (Galston, 2001). Educators and government leaders agree on the importance of democratic education because of society's reliance on the people to make deliberate choices about the direction of their collective lives (Battistoni, 1985). Yet there is a range of terms used in the language to describe democratic development or civic engagement.

While an earlier notion of citizenship was simply to master a body of facts, a more recent idea is that citizenship should mean active participation with rigorous interpersonal discussion (Battistoni, 1985). Gibson (2001), writing for the Carnegie Foundation, explains that "the heart of a healthy democracy is a citizenry actively engaged in civic life—taking responsibility for building communities, solving community problems, and participating in the electoral and political processes" (Gibson, 2001, p. 1).

Historically, the public school has emerged as the agent of citizenship education—a natural place to acculturate a common set of ideas and ideals to preserve social cohesion and solidarity (Battistoni, 1985). In reality, a variety of agents influence youth civic engagement, including schools, parental education, family communication practices, and feelings of social trust (Flanagan & Faison, 2001). Those who are concerned with civic engagement are divided among themselves as to the best strategies for increasing engagement and the outcomes that might constitute success (Fields, 2003). Many experts believe that an integrated approach to increasing youth civic engagement would work best, an approach that combines experiences such as civic education, service learning, political action or advocacy, and youth development (Fields, 2003).

Out-of-school time and youth development programs can fill a significant role in promoting civic engagement and democracy skill building. Schools are clearly not the only avenue through which children and adolescents learn about civic and democratic processes. Because of their unique characteristics as youth-serving organizations, out-of-school time programs, and in this case debate clubs, can provide critical opportunities for young people to nurture and practice democracy skills.

PROGRAM CONTEXT AND DESIGN

Urban Debate Leagues primarily function as out-of-school time programs engaging youth participation during the hours after school and on weekends. Youth turnout for urban debate programs has grown steadily since the 9.3-million-dollar seed funding initiative by the Soros Foundation in 1997. Youth debate programs are thriving in New York City, Baltimore, Seattle, Los Angeles, Chicago, and other urban centers and encompass more than 260 urban public high school and middle schools with over 12,000 young people participating since 1997. Both the academically high achieving and the academically struggling are encouraged to participate in debate.

The IMPACT Coalition, a nonprofit mentoring and educational development organization, manages the New York Urban Debate League (NYUDL). The NYUDL was established in 1997 in partnership with the Barkley Forum and the Open Society Institute (OSI). The NYUDL was begun with the goal of making debate, and specifically policy debate, accessible to all city students across race and socioeconomic class. NYUDL teams gather in over seventy schools with over 450 youth participants. It is the largest youth urban debate league in the country.

Debate is an activity sponsored and organized on a national level by the National Forensic League (NFL). The NFL sets the rules and regulations for debate competition. School debate teams compete in debate tournaments organized by their local leagues and travel to "invitational" tournaments held around the country. With a focus on "policy debate" the NYUDL gives New York City students access to participation in a national activity in which students from around the country debate the same national resolution (for example, that the United States federal government should establish a foreign policy substantially increasing its support of United Nations' peacekeeping operations). Debate contests typically consist of pairs of students arguing the affirmative and negative case of the resolution. Debate teams prepare both arguments because assignments will rotate.

The IMPACT Coalition provides teachers and students from selected high schools with intensive summer training in policy debate, weekend tournament competitions, ongoing mentoring, debate materials and curricular resources, scholarships to national summer debate camps, and special end-of-year culminating events. Resources provided by the NYUDL include a coaching manual, debate guides, summer debate institute, and Web-based training materials.

Debate programs typically enroll middle and high school youth. The National Forensic League and the Urban Debate Leagues offer regional and national competition at these grade levels. However, older elementary students may enjoy and benefit from participation in a noncompetitive school debate club with an emphasis on building research and oral presentation skills. While most debate teams tend to meet in school buildings, using classroom and library space, community-based settings can also work.

Staff

The most important resource for establishing a successful debate program is the coach. A wide range of individuals serve as debate coaches, including college students, teachers, AmeriCorp volunteers, and other professionals. Many former high school and college debaters seek out opportunities to stay involved with debate. Youth learn the art, language, and culture of debate through a coach. The coaches also provide youth with mentors and role models.

Program Activities

Some teams meet every afternoon after school; others two to three days a week. Some school-based teams are fortunate to have an elective school period for debate practice. More typically, teams meet in school buildings as afterschool clubs or in community organizations in the hours following school. When students arrive to practice debating, they work on writing blocks (arguments), note taking, vocabulary, researching, and speed vocal drills. They get help from other experienced debaters on various strategies and skills. They are often broken into smaller groups to work on weak areas and review evidence. The debate coach engages the youth in a range of activities using a variety of coaching and teaching techniques.

How often the team debates will depend on the level of engagement in local, regional, or national tournaments. New teams tend to compete with other local teams. As a team matures and becomes more experienced and sophisticated at debate, the level of competition sought may increase. Success at local and regional tournaments may lead to invitations to compete at the national tournament level.

Often, teams will spend the entire school year prepping and practicing for debate on the national resolution. Experience from the first debate competition of the school year will stimulate new thinking on evidence and arguments. With each new debate tournament, teams refine their debate presentation while polishing presentation style and skills. Coaches describe a rigorous level of preparation prior to tournament participation:

> We practice authentic experiences. We use practice debate to pinpoint the merits and weaknesses of their arguments and presentations. We debate as usual but break it up by adding debriefing sessions. (High School Debate Coach)

> Preparation depends on ability level. Advanced debaters write arguments for novices. The novices do less research and instead do more prep work for the debates. Novices practice the best ways to incorporate arguments; then they read and reread materials. Advanced debaters write blocks for opposing arguments (lots of research) and often visit the Brooklyn Resource Center. (High School Debate Coach)

ACADEMIC STANDARDS

The activities and skills that youth gain as they participate in urban debate connect directly to learning standards. Democracy skill-building activities such as urban debate stretch across the syllabus, including learning standards covered in English language arts and social studies. Urban debate can serve as a vehicle to bring these different strands together in meaningful ways that communicate both the content and responsibilities of democracy.

One of the standards that urban debate clearly supports is the New York State English Language Arts Standard #3:

> Students will listen, speak, read, and write for critical analysis and evaluation. As listeners and readers, students will analyze experiences, ideas, information, and issues presented by others using a variety of established criteria. As speakers and writers, they will use oral and written language that follows the accepted conventions of

the English language to present, from a variety of perspectives, their opinions and judgments on experiences, ideas, information and issues. (New York State Academy for Teaching and Learning, n.d.)

In addition, the debate experience also is aligned with New York State Social Studies Standard #5:

Students will use a variety of intellectual skills to demonstrate their understanding of the necessity for establishing governments; the governmental system of the United States and other nations; the United States Constitution; the basic civic values of American constitutional democracy; and the roles, rights, and responsibilities of citizenship, including avenues of participation. (New York State Academy for Teaching and Learning, n.d.)

Participation in debate supports these learning standards through daily activities that include reading newspapers and other nonfiction materials. In addition, participants conduct research utilizing library and Internet resources. They learn about and discuss current political and social issues. They develop written opinions, essays, and summary statements about the issues.

Students develop language and literacy skills by practicing oral presentation as well as practicing active listening and critiquing others' oral presentations. Participants develop critical-thinking skills by using logic and reasoning, constructing arguments, as well as developing strategies for debate competitions. What debate coaches most bank on is seeing an increase in youth's critical-thinking skills. The young people themselves describe many skill-based benefits from their participation in debate:

I have become a lot more comfortable with presentations in class. At school, we have to present a portfolio. We have to write really persuasive arguments in a short amount of time. We spend a lot of time building our arguments—debate helped me writing essays using the same techniques, going through evidence, using that to prove something. (High School Debater)

Finally, rather than relying on tests, students receive the benefit of ongoing self-evaluation and constructive criticism from their peers and coaches, which provides a level of efficacy within and control over the learning process.

YOUTH DEVELOPMENT

Civic competency is a cornerstone of youth development. A body of work has begun to build upon and expand the notion of civic competency

(Niemi & Chapman, 1999, p. 9). These capacities are imbedded in and aligned with the youth development assets outlined by the National Research Council (2002). This crossover between youth development assets and civic engagement capacities confirms the value of considering the powerful connections between participation in democracy skill building and positive youth development. The following is a discussion of some of the civic competencies addressed by this project.

Social Purpose and Affiliation With Society

While discussions about current events are likely to come up in typical school classrooms, "owning" an issue as one does in debate prompts a different type of intellectual and emotional understanding. In order to argue the affirmative or negative case, the debater has to take in the issue—know it as his or her own. We have been struck by how meaningful debate becomes for participants. One of the middle school debaters offered, "It's our democracy and not George Bush's democracy or Bill Clinton's democracy, or even George Washington's democracy or Abe Lincoln's democracy; it's our democracy, and that's what counts."

A high school junior recalled how participation in debate gave her a greater sense of purpose. The peacekeeping debates had struck a cord. The student felt inspired by her debate investigation and moved to bring her opinions to a bigger stage. She and debate friends prepared a more formal presentation of their debate ideas and arguments and made a trip to the United Nations. They believed strongly enough in the solutions and suggestions they had dutifully researched and debated to want to share them in the most real and substantial forum. Their actions clearly demonstrate the personal impact debate had on their lives and the connections they made between the larger public democracy and their civic identities and responsibilities.

Connection Between Public Political Process and Private Lives

Debate topics are national or global and immediately challenge the participants to think beyond the confines of their own families, schools, and communities. Yet, at the same time, topics lead the debater to consider the local implications and reflect on how global issues also relate to the home community. For example, in the spring of 2005 debaters considered a resolution that "the United States federal government should establish a foreign policy substantially increasing its support of United Nations peacekeeping operations." According to program leaders, it didn't take much for youth to recognize that commitment of United States forces has an obvious local effect as more soldiers, particularly from poor communities, are recruited and assigned to cover U.S. obligations oversees.

Program leaders say that youth debaters feel an increased sense of civic responsibility. Participants say they want to use their political skills, want to vote, and hope to get into the political life of the community. Having participated in debate, some youth have started their own community service projects related to debate issues. One coach summarizes that participation in debate "allows for the making of substantial connections between school classes, the news, debate topics, personal values/ethics, and broad social concepts."

Understanding Democracy and Civic Participation

In order to participate in debate, young people must become knowledgeable about forms of government and be able to incorporate relevant information into their debate content. Through debate activities, they are practicing a key component of civic participation—gaining knowledge. Boston Debate League leader Laura Sjoberg refers to the type of learning the students get out of participation in urban debate as "real time learning." Students have the opportunity to learn about political issues that are related to the here and now—they are engaged in investigating and preparing information about current issues and topics.

Preparing to debate requires collecting information from various sources, analyzing and organizing the information, and articulating a point of view. One high school coach reflected how on "a daily basis I scaffold learning so we can build upon the basics and begin thinking critically about the subject matter." The very nature of debate affirms the value of diverse opinions and dialogue, which are central to our understanding of democracy.

Support for Authority and Willingness to Dissent

It would come as no surprise to hear middle or high school students disagreeing with any authoritatively imposed rules or policies. Current literature notes the high level of cynicism young people express about the federal government and public policies (Flanagan & Faison, 2001; Soule, 2001). Finding the balance between supporting authoritative structures and also constructively articulating opposing opinions is challenging. One of the enriching aspects of participation in youth debate is learning the language of political criticism. Not only do debaters have to be able to defend both sides of an opinion, but also their arguments need to be constructive and persuasive. They learn the skill of using language for positive conflict resolution. Debaters find a voice for dissent and an ability to craft that voice in ways that are respectful, valued, and heard by others.

Capacity for Autonomous Choices and Decisions

Debate teams are student centered and self-sufficient. Several of the coaches suggested that the students really manage the program. It is not difficult to make the association between the skills that debate hones and the capacity for autonomous choice. Additionally, once a debate begins, decision-making skills are crucial. The debater's ability to listen, organize, and make informed decisions on debate strategy and approach is critical to team success. For these decisions debaters are on their own.

Engagement in Shared Discourse
Tolerant of Other Opinions

Shared discourse is the foundation of debate. A standard debate tournament structure means that a team rotates, arguing both the negative and affirmative opinion. A high school debater shared that she and a teammate "argued both opinions so many times that we became very open to accepting both opinions." The process of investigating, preparing, and arguing opposing opinions provides a unique experience to debaters, beyond the traditional experience of preparing a persuasive essay that expresses only one opinion.

We found that middle school debaters had a great zest for shared discourse. While accepting of other opinions, they were lured by the thrill of persuading others to their convictions.

> If somebody goes against what I am saying, I just pull out more facts and more facts to let them know that I am right. And [I] speak out clearly. So they'll know "he's aggressive and he's got his facts straight, so I can say nothing about it and I got to agree." What you have to do in a debate is make sure you are very clear, that you understand what you are arguing and why you are arguing it. Sometimes you have to make a compromise. (Middle School Debater)

Respect for Others and the
Groups to Which They Belong

Youth who are involved in debate like the social aspects of debate team participation. Debate tournaments are held throughout the city, which necessitates visiting other areas outside of home neighborhoods and meeting youth from other parts of the city. As teams improve, their tournament schedule may take them to regional and national competitions. Teams of debaters can meet frequently over the course of a season. While competitive feelings exist, there is also, as one debater explains, a respect that develops for other teams and other programs:

> On a personal level, not actually debating, I learned so much from everyone. I am able to see classism and racism in new ways— through exposure to so many different people, situations, and experiences. (High School Debater)

Leadership

Youniss et al. (2002) note that putting in hours toward a political cause or a service activity has only limited meaning unless change happens within the individual and that change is understood. It is typical that former high school debaters, now college students, volunteer as judges in competitions. High school practice sessions are frequented by alumni debaters who assist advanced debaters in writing arguments while novice debaters focus on oral practice.

Many coaches we interviewed had experience as high school or college debaters. A former debater, now a law student in Boston, recently founded the Boston Debate League. Debate participation that transcends graduations and college or career shifts speaks to the strength of the association many young people feel with the urban debate leagues and attests to the change that debate effects within participants. Debate alumni consistently credit debate experiences with their success in higher education as well as with influencing their career choices and achievements.

Belief in Ability to Make a Difference

It is necessary to convey to participants in debate that they are valued and contributing members of a community. Urban debate leaders view themselves as agents of change working toward the development of more informed and actively engaged young citizens. Program leaders in the Baltimore Urban Debate League (UDL) deliberately promote the conscious link between developing skills and transferring those skills back into the improvement of participants' own lives and communities. Baltimore UDL extends experiences for youth beyond the debate tournament by sponsoring debate exhibitions at venues such as popular open markets and city hall. It's a reminder to participants that debate is about real people and real life.

Youth and coaches spoke about their beliefs in the ability to influence change:

> I think that I am more likely to speak about controversial things in class. More likely to help other people, to think that I can help people with other things. I am not necessarily smarter or better because of debate, but may be in a better position to help. (High School Debater)

> Through debate youth are shown how their voice can make a difference, and how to argue their point of view productively. The most important lesson they learn is not to give up, to set goals, and to put forth effort. They will continue debating and learn to articulate their voice. (High School Debate Coach)

SUMMARY

Research on the current status of youth civic engagement suggests the importance of moving an agenda forward that prepares young people to participate fully in our democracy as informed, competent, and responsible active citizens. The work of providing activities that engage youth in "democracy in action" will take enormous collective effort by schools, government agencies, youth-serving organizations, policy makers, religious organizations, and others. Programs such as the urban debate leagues serve as a dynamic and inspired model—one that has demonstrated its value to young urban youth and the broader community.

Replication in Other Contexts

Providing engaging civic and democracy development experiences such as debate during the out-of-school time hours is challenging. There are several infrastructure components necessary to support an active and successful debate team experience. On a smaller scale, with the commitment of an experienced coach, debate can be infused into a typical afterschool program as a club activity. Teams of youth from within the program can practice debating each other on selected topics. This practice can lead up to a formal debate in front of an audience that includes families, teachers, school administrators, and others from the school community. Potential sources for debate coaches include college debate teams, legal professionals, parents with prior experience in high school or college debate, and government or history teachers.

On a larger scale, debate clubs can connect to debate leagues, such as the NYUDL, and participate in national policy debate through membership in local, regional, or national leagues and tournaments. This more extensive debate model usually requires linkage to the school for physical space, technology and information resources, financial support for tournament travel (school bus), and expert team facilitation. Buy-in from a school principal is essential.

Steps to creating a new debate program:

1. Consider the scope of the debate program. Do you want it to be an internal project within a school or an afterschool program, or will it involve membership in a regional or national league?

2. Organize promotional materials about the history and value of debate. (See the many resources provided by the National Forensic League.)

3. Obtain necessary support from the school, community organizations, families, and other stakeholders. Assure access to meeting space and technology resources.

4. Recruit a debate coach or coaches (volunteer or paid) and youth participants.

(Continued)

(Continued)

5. Communicate participation guidelines and objectives.

6. Plan syllabus for issue investigation and debate preparation.

7. Solidify level of participation and other requirements—i.e., number of tournaments, locations, transportation, costs.

8. Make publicity connections with local newspapers and school and community newsletters to report on debate program activities.

9. Engage all stakeholders, including youth, coaches, parents, school personnel, government officials, and sponsors in a program sustainability strategy.

References

Battistoni, R. (1985). *Public schooling and the education of democratic citizens.* Jackson: University Press of Mississippi.

Dewey, J. (1916). *Democracy and education.* New York: Macmillan.

Fields, A. (2003). *The youth challenge: Participating in democracy.* New York: The Carnegie Corporation.

Flanagan, C., & Faison, N. (2001). Youth civic development: Implications of research for social policy and program. *Social Policy Report, 15,* 1.

Galston, W. (2001). *Political knowledge, political engagement, and civic education.* College Park: University of Maryland.

Gibson, C. (2001). *From inspiration to participation: A review of perspectives on youth civic engagement.* New York: The Carnegie Corporation.

National Research Council and Institute of Medicine, Committee on Community-Level Programs for Youth. (2002). *Community programs to promote youth development* (J. Eccles & J. A. Gootman, Eds.). Washington, DC: National Academy Press.

New York State Academy for Teaching and Learning. (n.d.). *New York State learning standards.* Retrieved March 11, 2007, from http://www.emsc.nysed.gov/nysatl/standards.html

Niemi, R. G., & Chapman, C. (1999). *The civic development of 9th through 12th grade students in the United States: 1966.* Washington, DC: National Center for Education Statistics.

Soule, S. (2001). *Will they engage?: Political knowledge, participation, and attitudes of generation x and y.* Calabasas, CA: Center for Civic Education.

Youniss, J., Bales, S., Christmas-Best, V., Diversi, M., McLaughlin, M., & Silbereisen, R. (2002). Youth civic engagement in the twenty-first century. *Journal of Research on Adolescence, 12*(1), 121–148.

RESOURCES

Daley, P., & Dahlie, M. S. (2001). *50 debate prompts for kids*. New York: Scholastic.

Davidson, J. (1997). *The middle school debater*. Bellingham, WA: Right Book Company.

Denver, D., & Hands, G. (1990). Does studying politics make a difference? The political knowledge, attitudes, and perceptions of school students. *British Journal of Political Science, 20*, 263–288.

Ericson, J. M., Murphy, J. J., & Zeuscher, R. F. (2003). *The debater's guide*. Carbondale, IL: Southern Illinois Press.

Fine, G. A. (2001). *Gifted tongues: High school debate and adolescent culture*. Princeton, NJ: Princeton University Press.

Freeley, A. J. (1999). *Argumentation and debate: Critical thinking for reasoned decision making*. Belmont, CA: Wadsworth Publishing.

International Debate Education Association (IDEA). (2004). *The debatabase: A must-have guide for successful debate*. New York: iDebate Press.

Meany, J., & Shuster, K. (2005). *Speak out! Debate and public speaking in the middle grades*. New York: International Debate Education Association.

Pearson, S., & Voke, H. (2003). *Building an effective citizenry: Lessons learned from initiatives in youth engagement*. Washington, DC: American Youth Policy Forum.

Ravitch, D., & Viteritti, J. (Eds.). (2001). *Making good citizens*. New Haven: Yale University Press.

Remy, R. C. (1980). *Handbook of basic citizenship competencies*. Alexandria, VA: Association of Supervision and Curriculum Development.

Torney-Purta, J. (2000). *Creating citizenship: Youth development for free and democratic society. Executive summary*. College Park: University of Maryland. (ERIC Document Reproduction Service No. ED 440 914).

Zompetti, J. P., Motiejunaite, J., Driscoll, W., & Bowker, J. (2005). *Discovering the world through debate: A practical guide to educational debate for debaters, coaches and judges* (3rd ed.). New York: International Debate Education Association.

Web Sites

Debate Outreach Network, www.debateoutreach.net

The International Debate Education Association, http://www.idebate.org

National Catholic Forensic League, www.ncfl.org

National Forensic League, www.nflonline.org

4

So You Want to Be a Superhero?

How the Art of Making Comics in an Afterschool Setting Develops Young People's Creativity, Literacy, and Identity

Sarita Khurana

One day while visiting a local bookstore, I walked past an aisle of graphic novels, how-to-draw books, and comic collections. To my surprise, I observed a group of teenagers sitting on the floor or leaning against the bookshelves, their backpacks in disarray around them. What were all these young people doing at 3:30 in the afternoon on a beautiful spring weekday in New York City? They were reading. This may come as a shock to those who believe the myth that young people don't like to read—certainly not outside of required school reading, certainly not after school when they could be playing basketball or video games. These young people were reading comics, a whole genre of reading material that fascinates and engages many young people.

When people think of comics, they imagine superheroes in colorful costumes fighting dastardly villains, cats chasing mice, or cuddly bunnies.

Comics have been defined as "juxtaposed pictorial and other images in deliberate sequence, intended to convey information and/or to produce an aesthetic response in the viewer" (McCloud, 1993, p. 9). By that definition, the epic story contained in a pre-Columbian picture manuscript telling of the great Mixtec military and political hero Eight Deer Tiger Claw would qualify as a comic. The Bayeux Tapestry, a 230-foot tapestry detailing the Norman conquest of England in 1066, as well as Egyptian paintings, Trajan's Column, Greek urn paintings, and Japanese scrolls would also qualify as comics. To that illustrious history, I would add comic art, one of the most popular storytelling media around the globe. From classic American comic strips to Japanese *Manga*, comics cover subjects ranging from humorous teen angst to social commentary.

Many afterschool programs have chosen to align themselves with youth culture, promoting activities to which young people are drawn, such as hip hop dance, photography, fashion clubs, and soccer. To that list we can add classes on making comics. Older youth, in particular, vote with their feet when it comes to regular participation in afterschool programs. Yet they are naturally drawn to making comics, excited to have a chance to draw their own characters and develop their own stories. After all, they've been reading comics for a long time, sometimes starting with newspaper comic strips, and they've been familiar with animated characters since they were introduced to Saturday morning cartoons and video games.

This chapter will describe a comic-making class offered at the Educational Alliance in New York City. In this class, comics are taken seriously, both as reading material and as an art medium. This chapter will demonstrate how participants are engaged in learning not only the craft of comic production—including storyline development, character profiles, sequential storytelling, and illustration—but also many of the skills that support academic outcomes, particularly in language arts. In addition, the chapter will show how this endeavor is grounded in positive youth development and can help youth explore and establish their own individual and collective identities.

THEORETICAL FRAMEWORK

There is a growing body of research on the use of popular and youth culture, such as comics and the Internet (including sometimes controversial Web sites such as myspace.com), as a source of literacy development and identity exploration for older youth (Alvermann, 2002; Bitz, 2006; Hull, Kenny, Marple, & Forsman-Schneider 2006; Schultz, Brockenbrough, & Dhillon, 2005). This work has examined how young people's use of cultural tools reveals their view of the world and their values. In addition, the research is examining how the use of cultural tools provides opportunities for growth as readers and writers.

In her work on children's use of media and popular cultural symbols, Anne Dyson writes, "[C]hildren may position themselves within stories that reveal dominant ideological assumptions about categories of individuals and the relations between them—boys and girls, adults and children, rich people and poor, people of varied heritages, physical demeanors, and societal powers" (Dyson, 1996, p. 472). In his book on the art of cartoons, McCloud (1993) explains that "entering the world of the cartoon, you see yourself . . . through factors such as universal identification, simplicity, and childlike features of characters" (McCloud, 1993, p. 57). The cartoon "is a vacuum into which our identity and awareness are pulled . . . an empty shell that we inhabit which enables us to travel in another realm. We don't just observe the cartoon, we become it . . ." (McCloud, 1993, p. 57).

Additional research on the development of multiple literacies is showing that people acquire literacy through a range of opportunities and multiple points of entry, many of which do not occur during school time (Hull & Schultz, 2002). The afterschool time is an important space where this can go on because it has traditionally allowed opportunities for creative and artistic exploration, unhindered by a narrow focus on an academic curriculum or upon grade achievement. Shirley Brice Heath (2001) writes, "For some children and youth [afterschool programming] fosters a sense of self-worth and a host of talents—particularly linguistic and creative—that classrooms neither have the time nor legal permission to foster" (p. 10).

PROGRAM CONTEXT AND DESIGN

The Educational Alliance, an old settlement house in the Lower East Side of New York City, serves children and families, providing such services as Head Start, afterschool programs, and mental health programs. School of the Future, a public middle and high school in Manhattan, has partnered with the Alliance for the past seven years, housing the Alliance's afterschool program. The Educational Alliance's partnership with the School of the Future complements the school day by providing young people with enrichment opportunities they do not usually get in school. The Alliance has received most of its program funding from public sources, including New York State's Office of Children & Family Services, The After School Corporation, and, most recently, the New York City Department of Youth and Community Development.

Students at School of the Future are sixth to twelfth graders drawn from neighborhoods all over the city—a diverse mix of African American, Latino, Asian, and white students. Of the 550 students enrolled in the school, approximately 300 are part of the daily afterschool program, which runs from Monday–Friday, 3–6 PM. Of course, some students attend the program because their parents need a place for them to be after school, while parents are at work, but many students attend the program because they like what's offered: arts, technology, sports, academics, and recreation. Students select their own afterschool classes each semester and receive elective school credit for regularly participating in and completing the classes. This credit helps build connections with the school day and provides recognition of the learning students do after school. All the classes use an approach called project-based learning, whose final products include performances, writing, and visual art displays.

The afterschool program is run by a full-time site-based director, who is employed by the Educational Alliance and supervises about forty part-time staff and volunteers. Each day, students who stay for the afterschool program transition from their school day into the afterschool snack period, followed by forty-five minutes of quiet time for homework and other school assignments. Once homework hour ends, students move into their afterschool classes. Classrooms used for eighth grade English and math during the day are now used for robotics, yoga, and comics in the afternoon.

The afterschool comics class was started at School of the Future in the autumn of 2001 and has been a regular offering since then. To find instructors, Program Director Mitzi Sinnott posted advertisements on craigslist .org on the Internet and sent e-mails to local art schools and comic book houses like Marvel and DC Comics in New York City. Through a contact at DC Comics, she found Alex Simmons, who, at the time of this writing, has been working in the afterschool setting for the past six years. His background is in the comics industry; he spent many years producing and writing his own work, *BlackJack,* a story about an African American soldier of fortune set in Tokyo in the mid-1930s. Alex and I spent quite a bit of time talking about his class and the comics industry in general. As an African American man, he is a veteran of the difficult race and class dynamics of the comics industry. Of the many afterschool educators and teaching artists that I know, Alex is one of the best. He cares deeply about his students and is extremely knowledgeable and passionate about his medium.

During the 2004 spring semester, there were fifteen students in the comics class, about two-thirds from middle school and the rest from high school. As many girls were enrolled in the class as boys; about half of the students were new to class, while the rest were reenrolled for at least a second semester.

Program Activities

A typical day in the comics class begins with a lot of chatter. Several students are already in the classroom before 3 P.M., pulling out their sketchpads and notebooks, as the rest of the students filter in from snack time. On one particular day, Hillary and Wynonah, two middle school girls already seated close together, are busily updating each other on what's happened in their comic stories since last week's class: Wynonah's animal characters in her cartoon "Hamsterville" have run away from home and arrived in New York City; Hillary is still working on sketching her main character, Gladiator Girl. Most of the students sit in twos and threes, working and talking even before Alex has officially started the three-hour class. Others sit by themselves, usually wearing headphones, working in their own musical space. Someone always brings in a new comic book to show or has a story to tell about a character's latest adventure.

Like any other written medium, comic-book storytelling has its own conventions. Students begin by learning the basic elements of the page: panel, thought-bubble, speech balloon, and caption box. Other basics are visual rather than written: e.g., drawing the human body or learning perspective. Ultimately, students learn how to use both images and words to construct complex stories.

Since not all students have drawing skills, the first fifteen minutes of class is usually an exercise in one-minute sketching. Two students volunteer to be models, while the rest tell them how to pose. For instance, when Wynonah and Hassan volunteered, the rest of the class called out action poses: "You guys have to act like . . . Hassan is riding a horse, and Wynonah, you're on the floor in pain." "OK, both of you pretend you're doing a *Matrix* pose like jumping between buildings." Then they switch to two new volunteers: "OK, Jake, you're dancing, and Mia, you're sitting in a yoga pose near his feet." "Jake, you lie down, and Mia, you stand up and pretend you're going to kick him in the stomach" (class exercise, February 10, 2004). These exercises get students to see the world from different angles and help them with their drawing styles. Students work on basic drawing techniques such as line, shape, color, and perspective. They can have their classmates pose in stances that occur in their storyline, so they can practice drawing something that is relevant to their work. Sometimes Alex asks the students to make a one-minute sketch into a comic strip, so the drawing practice becomes an exercise in sequential storytelling.

When sketching time is over, students get down to work on their projects. New students begin with three- or four-panel comic strips like those in newspapers. Even a three-panel strip requires a storyline; it has to have a beginning, middle, and end. Students need to think about elements of story structure: What is the genre—science fiction, adventure, fantasy? Who are the characters? What is the mood—humorous, serious, or suspenseful? What is the point of the story? What are the first and last shots the audience will see, and what's in the middle? Sal's first four-panel comic strip about Electro Magnetic Man introduced the character, who is shown being zapped by telephone wires. The last panel shows him with electric yellow zigzag hair and a bolt of lightning coming out of his left hand, announcing, "I'm Electro Magnetic Man!" This may not seem like the kind of writing students have to do in English class, but they are learning to use such basic literary elements as dialogue, plot, character, and theme.

Once students feel comfortable developing a basic comic strip, they can move on to more elaborate work. One option is to develop their initial strip into a series. Alex asks students to think of themselves as comic artists producing for a daily newspaper, so that they make a new comic strip for every class and complete a whole series within a semester. Malcolm, a sixth grader new to the class, is working on a series called "Fowl Prey," in which a group of birds conspire to conquer the world. The first strip shows a group of seven or eight birds meeting in the basement of a house, establishing their purpose: to rid the city of other gangs. By the end of the spring semester, Malcolm has produced eight "Fowl Prey" comic strips. The birds have come a long way in carrying out their dastardly plot—and Malcolm has come an equally long way in his ability to use the elements of narrative.

Another option for students is to develop their own comic book. Newer students usually work on producing a four-page comic book, while more seasoned students may produce a complete twenty-two-page comic. The process is the same, and Alex has a way of breaking it down into manageable chunks. Like many good afterschool educators, he starts where the students are—with their interests, enthusiasm, and ideas. This practice of engaging young people, taking their skill level into account, is central to good youth development.

Character and Story Development

Comic book production begins with developing a profile sheet for the main character: What is her motivation and background? What are the main events in her life? Linta, another sixth grader, shows me the profile sheet for her character, Muoliko, drawn in full Japanese *Manga* style and personality. It reads: "Muoliko—she is turned into a half-cat for stealing and eating someone's magic red bean cakes. She eats them and is kicked out of her house by her sister because her younger brother is allergic to red bean cakes. She takes care of herself. Muoliko tries to find a way to undo the spell. Tomboyish, age 11, comes from the planet Copiko" (interview, April 28, 2004).

Next, students write pitch sheets similar to the ones professional comic artists use to present their work to prospective employers. In this storyline summary, students are not yet working on the exact details, but they have a good idea of the story structure as a whole. Next come script layouts: thumbnails of each page of the comic book. This is the step in which students work out the details of their story. A script layout can take a student an entire semester to produce because it includes a rough sketch not only of text but also of images.

Together, these pieces—character profile sheet, pitch sheet, and script layout—make up a professional presentation package. With this completed, students could easily go to a comic book industry representative with a portfolio of their work and "pitch" their comic book idea. Once the presentation package is complete, students move on to actually writing, drawing, inking, lettering, and coloring the entire comic.

ACADEMIC STANDARDS

Comic storytelling is a rich medium with which afterschool practitioners can build and expand the skills and knowledge students learn during the school day. The teacher of the comics class, Alex, makes regular reference to what is taught in language arts, English, social studies, science, and history classes. He has students work up single-panel political cartoons, which present opportunities to discuss current events and politics. Students develop and apply what they learn in school in new ways, putting Greek mythology or their fifth-period science experiment into their comics. Of course, they also draw on popular culture references and their own experiences. Whether they're working from television, the latest video game, or someone they know, ultimately the class is about narrative—telling stories in visual and literal form.

Engaging young people in comic production is a clever way to help them work on language arts skills. A look at the four New York State English language arts standards reveals how comics can enhance literacy instruction:

Standard 1: Students will read, write, listen, and speak for information and understanding.

Standard 2: Students will read, write, listen, and speak for literary response and expression.

Standard 3: Students will read, write, listen, and speak for critical analysis and evaluation.

Standard 4: Students will read, write, listen, and speak for social interaction. (New York State Education Department, 1996)

Each of these standards is addressed in producing comics. A comic artist must process information by sequencing the plot of a comic before writing it, as demonstrated in students' development of a character profile sheet and script layouts. Comic art is an expressive, interpretive art form with a long history of techniques and aesthetics; students need to work within this tradition and interpret how the images and text work together to tell the story. In order to tell a comic story effectively, the artist must analyze and evaluate the underlying meaning of the story. The artist must also interact socially with other readers; students often discuss their work in small groups in the comics class. Reading skill is also addressed, as students read various publications, explore different genres, and learn new vocabulary as background preparation for their own creations. Students often revise their work with the help of the instructor, going through several drafts to produce the final version. This emphasis on comprehension and revision supports both their reading and writing.

In one example of this, the student Hassan came up with a character for his comic because he loves Samurai movies. But when challenged by the instructor to figure out his character's life, Hassan had to do some research to fill in the gaps in his knowledge. Where did Samurais come from? How were they raised—in a noble family, as peasants? How were they trained? Alex starts the exploratory process by asking students what they know about history and mythology, so they start by building on their own knowledge base. Then Alex helps students find appropriate books to use as references and encourages them to use the Web to look up the relevant historical period and read about the places they want to use as settings.

In another example, as Sal worked on his Electro Magnetic Man comic strip, I asked him to describe what was happening. "In the first panel, that's a U.S. battle ship patrolling the waters. In the second panel, that's Napoleon sailing in an old forty-eight-gunner ship, and it's about to attack the U.S. ship." "OK, wait," I say, "How do you know so much about ships" (interview, May 4, 2004)? I found out that Sal is a big fan of ships, and not only from watching the movie *Master and Commander.* He told me about a collection of books about Horatio Hornblower and the British Royal Navy. Although these books are too advanced for him to read, his love of ships has inspired him to listen to the books on tape. Reading them himself is certainly in his future.

YOUTH DEVELOPMENT

A comics art class has the potential to capitalize on several youth development opportunities, from helping young people develop literacy skills to grappling with adolescent identity issues. Some outstanding ways that a comics class can support youth development include career exploration, which, by definition, includes a vision for the future. In addition, the class helps young people develop and practice problem solving and conflict resolution skills.

Vision for the Future

Alex helps students connect with the larger world of the comic book industry and gives them room to envision themselves as professional comic artists. In the comics class, young people explore all sides of the comic book industry. They learn the various roles, such as penciler, writer, inker, editor, colorist, and letterer; sometimes they practice these roles on each other's work, similar to the way production is broken down in the comics industry. Students also get a sense of what the world of comics is like by taking trips to the Museum of Cartoon and Comic Art (MoCCA), to cartoon film festivals, or to comic book publication houses such as DC Comics or Marvel Comics.

By linking the comics class to career development, instructors give young people an opportunity to think about their work in a larger context. The instructors also help young people develop a portfolio of their completed work, emulating the process of professional graphic artists in the field. Whether it is comic art, graphic design, filmmaking, writing children's books, or working for Sesame Street—there are a host of ways to link young people's interest in comic production to the professional world. Ultimately, this gives young people a sense of purpose and future.

Problem Solving and Conflict Resolution

Comic creation also entails a degree of conflict resolution and the ability to make choices. As they create a story, young people have to solve problems as well as make choices. I have often seen young people grapple with what direction their characters should take, and how they struggle with the consequences of their characters' actions. Such choices push young people to develop problem-solving skills through having to think abstractly and engage in reflection. They have to come up with alternative solutions for both cognitive and social problems. The creation of comics is a practice arena for these competencies, which can be used in other aspects of the youth's lives.

OTHER BENEFITS AND COMPETENCIES

Multiple Points of Entry Into Literacy

Comic book reading can serve as one of many possible points of entry into literacy. Sometimes students who are failing in school-based literacy activities can shine when they are engaged in literacy activities for which they have a passion. When I asked Hassan how long he'd been reading comics, he said that he'd been into comics since he was five: "Yeah, I used to play lots of video games, and my dad wanted me to learn to read, so he gave me comic books to read like the original Batman and Superman. . . . That helped me be more interested in reading and give it a try" (interview, May 4, 2004).

The varieties of comic books and graphic novels are as diverse as those within any literature, spanning genres such as science fiction, fantasy, and adventure to teen romance and humor. One interesting literary phenomenon has been the introduction of Japanese *Manga*. While, in the West, mainstream comics are almost entirely for children and adolescents, in Japan, many different types of *Manga* are written for people of all ages and both genders. It is not uncommon to see a middle-aged man reading *Manga* on the subway. While the average American comic is 22 pages long, the average *Manga* comic has 350 pages and contains as many as fifteen chapters.

The introduction of *Manga* in the United States has opened up a whole new audience for comics: girls. The comic industry in America has always been geared for a white male audience; the vast majority of comic superhero characters are white males. There is, however, a whole genre of *Manga* written specifically for girls. Such *Manga* as *Love Hina* and *Pitaten* are written with strong female leads. Partly because of the popularity of *Manga,* at least half of the comics class at Educational Alliance is usually female, and many of the female students' characters reflect the strong female characters found in Japanese comics.

Adolescent Identity Development

Producing comics not only supports young people's literacy development but also promotes their identity development. As young people grapple with questions of identity during adolescence, the production of comics in afterschool programs offers them a unique way to enter into an imagined world that allows them to experiment in safety. Inventing characters and storylines is a way for young people to express feelings, play out likes and dislikes, make choices, and test new ideas.

Eva, a ninth grader, was in her third year in the comics class. She developed a complete twenty-two-page comic book about Night Shade, a sixteen-year-old girl whose father was murdered by a police officer. Because the family is poor, Night Shade's father resorts to burglary in order to care for himself and his daughter. On one such expedition, an alarm gets tripped, and a police officer is called. Somehow, too much force is used, and Night Shade arrives on the scene to see her father beaten to death by the police officer. Night Shade swears to avenge her father's death by tracking down this police officer. As she has no means of survival, she does what she knows best—she steals. Inevitably, she is caught and sent to prison. There she meets a woman scientist who promises to give her superpowers if Night Shade will, on her release, seek revenge against the scientist's assistant who gave her up to the authorities. With this pact, Night Shade gains powers Eva describes as "speed, strength, agility, and aim. Her secret weapon is the ability to use night shade, a poison that she can draw from her veins and inject into others" (interview, April 28, 2004). When Night Shade gets out of prison, she goes on a quest to find first the scientist's enemy and then her father's killer. Eva's first full-length comic ends at the point at which Night Shade has tracked down the scientist's assistant and is face to face with him in a late-night brawl in his laboratory.

All of the main characters in student comics are transformed with new powers. Many have been abandoned or orphaned by a parent's accidental or murderous death, others are kicked out of their homes or have run away. Many characters adopt new families or friends along the way, usually someone who helps the main character develop his or her new powers and identity. This parallels adolescents' own desire to become empowered and explore their world. Through their characters, these young people try on new identities and imagine the possible worlds that they, themselves, can occupy. In this moment, the young people are figuring themselves out and making meaning of their world. In creating their own characters—from the kind of personality they have to the clothes they wear, the time periods they occupy, and the adventures they seek—these young artists and writers are defining a world of their own choosing.

Shirley Brice Heath (2001) writes that young people's art helps them resist their usual role assignments in the "real" world. Students' characters can be independent in the comic world, making choices that may not be available to authors in their real lives, at least not until they are adults. For young people, who are usually marginalized in adult society, expressing themselves in artistic possibility, in imagined and futuristic scenarios, is a healthy exploration of and sometime rejection of stereotypical societal role assignments.

Social Critique

Eva's Night Shade illustrates how the vehicle of comics provides young people with an opportunity to explore and challenge their own social realities through reading and writing. Eva's comic clearly takes issue with police brutality; it is a complex look at issues of power, class, and gender—issues Eva confronts in her daily life. Some of Eva's friends in school are young men of color who typically face harassment by the police. Eva uses the experience of her friends and her knowledge of the world in her comic book. She has subverted the traditional role of the police officer as "good guy" to reveal both her critique of institutional power and how she grapples with issues of police brutality and the abuse of power and privilege.

Students' appropriation of *Manga* characters or Samurai warriors is also a challenge to the world of the traditional male superhero. When I asked Hassan to describe Hazara, he said, "Well, he kind of reflects my personality—he can be serious, and he can get into trouble. He's kind of irresponsible, but a good leader, and likes to fight" (interview, May 4, 2004). Having gotten to know Hassan, I was not surprised to hear that he related personally to the characters he was creating. The previous semester, he had created, for the end-of-year visual arts display, a dreadlocked superhero that he said was based on himself, "but someone with powers." Students' characters take on new identities of race, class, gender, and culture, often morphing all of these in ways that extend or parallel the struggles in their communities and in their own lives.

SUMMARY

Adolescents are in the midst of a soul-searching process of identity development and are at a time when their interest in books and writing often wanes. In afterschool settings, a comics production class provides a safe, creative space where young people can test limits, exploring their worlds in outrageous and playful ways while at the same time developing literacy interests and abilities that support academic learning.

The semester ends with the students showing their work in the school's second floor display cabinets as part of the end-of-year afterschool visual arts show. Alex had made the students' comics into an *ashcan,* a magazine of comic art, which was copied for students to take home. Many of the students sign up for the comics class again to continue working on their pieces or to start new projects. Some will continue to inhabit their comic worlds over the summer, catching up on their favorite comic books or continuing to work on their original stories. The comics class has been a fun and productive way for students to spend their Wednesday afternoons, as well as a semester of learning, expanding literacy skills, and exploring new worlds.

Replication in Other Contexts

There are many ways to adapt the program to your own afterschool setting. Ideally, a good teaching artist is key—someone who has worked in the comic book field as an illustrator or writer. You want to be sure that the person you hire is versed in the comic medium as well as a good teacher. Some places you might want to post for an instructor are at the art departments of local colleges and universities or with local comic book houses such as DC Comics and Marvel Comics in New York City. The Director of School of the Future contacted DC Comics in New York and was led to Alex, who did some freelance writing for them and had previously worked with local youth groups. Each instructor will have his or her own ideas about the design of a comic book curriculum.

If finding a qualified instructor proves to be difficult, there are ways to introduce comic art into the afterschool setting on a smaller scale. Buy one of the many books listed in the Resources section that give you step-by-step instructions on drawing comics. These books outline the basics—from supplies you'll need like pencils and drawing paper to ideas for exercises to get young people thinking about and creating comic art.

The focus of a comics class doesn't have to be on teaching the students how to draw. Young people have a range of styles and will find a way to draw whatever is in their imagination. Youth comic art, and even professional comic art, ranges from simple stick-figure drawings to highly stylized and anatomically correct characters. While Alex is skilled in teaching youth the fundamentals of drawing and anatomy, the key is in working with young people to develop an idea into a story. You can start with the most basic idea of developing a character. If time is limited, the class can develop a collective character.

References

Alvermann, D. (2002). Effective literacy instruction for adolescents. *Journal of Literacy Research, 34*(2), 189–208.

Bitz, M. (2006, Fall). The art of democracy, democracy as art: Creative learning in afterschool comic book clubs. In *Afterschool Matters* (Occasional Paper No. 7, pp. 1–20). New York: The Robert Bowne Foundation.

Dyson, A. (1996) Cultural constellations and childhood identities: On Greek gods, cartoon heroes, and the social lives of schoolchildren. *Harvard Educational Review, 66*(3), 471–495.

Heath, S. B. (2001) Three's not a crowd: Plans, roles and focus in the arts. *Educational Researcher, 30*(7), 10–17.

Hull, G., & Schultz, K. (Eds.). (2002). *School's out! Bridging out-of-school literacies with classroom practice.* New York: Teachers College Press.

Hull, G., Kenney, N. L., Marple, S., & Forsman-Schneider, A. (2006, Spring). Many versions of masculine: An exploration of boys' identity formation through digital storytelling in an afterschool program. *Afterschool Matters* (Occasional Paper No. 6). New York: The Robert Bowne Foundation.

McCloud, S. (1993). *Understanding comics: The invisible art.* New York: Paradox Press

New York State Education Department. (1996). *Learning standards for English language arts.* Albany, NY: Author. (ERIC Document Reproduction Service No. ED400557)

Schultz, K., Brockenbrough, E., & Dhillon, J. (2005, Spring). In between work and school: Youth perspectives of an urban afterschool multimedia literacy program. In *Afterschool Matters* (Occasional Paper No. 4, pp. 1–18). New York: The Robert Bowne Foundation.

RESOURCES

Books

Caldwell, B. (2004). *Action cartooning.* New York: Sterling.

Caputo, T. C. (2002). *Visual storytelling: The art and technique.* New York: Watson-Guptill Publications.

Chiarello, M., & Klein, T. (2004). *The DC comics guide to coloring and lettering comics.* New York: Watson-Guptill Publications.

Dunn, B. (2002). *How to draw Manga.* San Antonio, TX: Antarctic Press.

Hart, C. (2003). *Xtreme art: Draw Manga!* New York: Watson-Guptill Publications.

Lee, S., & Buscema, J. (1984). *How to draw comics the Marvel way.* New York: Fireside Press.

O'Neil, D. (2001). *The DC comics guide to writing comics.* New York: Watson-Guptill Publications.

Smith, A. (2000). *Drawing dynamic comics.* New York: Watson-Guptill Publications.

Books on Anatomy

Gray, H. F. R. S. (1999). *Gray's Anatomy.* New York: Random House Value Publishing.

Hogarth, B. (1996). *Dynamic figure drawing*. New York: Watson-Guptill Publications.

Hogarth, B. (2003). *Dynamic anatomy*. New York: Watson-Guptill Publications.

Comic Book Medium

Eisner, W. (1995). *Comics and sequential art*. Tamarac, FL: Poorhouse Press.

Eisner, W. (1996). *Graphic storytelling*. Tamarac, FL: Poorhouse Press.

McCloud, S. (1994). *Understanding comics: The invisible art*. New York: Harper Paperbacks.

McCloud, S. (2000). *Reinventing comics: How imagination and technology are revolutionizing an art form*. New York: Harper Paperbacks.

Web Sites

The Comic Book Project, www.comicbookproject.org

The Comic Book Project is an arts-based literacy and learning initiative hosted by Teachers College, Columbia University with materials published by Dark Horse Comics. The goal of the project is to help children forge alternative pathways to literacy by writing, designing, and producing original comic books. Curriculum and lesson plans are available.

Museum of Cartoon and Comic Art (MoCCA), www.moccany.org

The purpose of the Museum of Comic and Cartoon Art, located in New York City, is the collection, preservation, study, and display of comic and cartoon art.

Association of Teaching Artists, www.teachingartists.com

This association hosts a listserv where you can post for teaching artists in a variety of disciplines in New York City.

DMOZ Open Directory Project: Comics Publishers, http://dmoz.org/Arts/Comics/Publishers/

Curious about checking out some comic books and graphic novels? There are so many great publishers—not just the big ones you hear about like DC and Marvel—but tons of independent publishers, with material for anyone on any subject. To check out a comprehensive list of publishers' Web sites, go to The Open Directory Project, the largest, most comprehensive human-edited directory of the Web. It is constructed and maintained by a vast, global community of volunteer editors.

5

Hair-Raising Experiences

"Doing Hair" and Literacy in an Afterschool Reading and Writing Workshop for African American Adolescent Girls

Daneell Edwards

"Doing hair" can refer to the simple acts of combing, brushing, washing, and styling. In the culture of adolescent African American girls, however, doing hair is a social practice that represents power, creativity, and sometimes popularity. Yet, African American girls' interest in hair is rarely recognized or embraced in school or supported in out-of-school settings.

Lisa Delpit (2002) argues that some African American children are not motivated to learn because materials presented to them do not connect to their own interests. In the course of her research, she observed girls grooming hair during school hours. Rather than ignore or berate them, she developed a multidisciplinary unit on the topic of hair that engaged the young people in rich language and literacy experiences that included interviewing hairstylists, creating linguistic maps of Africa, and using the Internet to learn about other cultures and time periods through the study of hair.

Building on the work of Delpit, I developed a reading and writing after-school workshop on hair for African American adolescent girls.

This chapter describes a three-month afterschool reading and writing workshop for African American adolescent girls that focused on doing hair. It was shaped by this question: "Can we learn from an afterschool program that affords African American adolescent girls the opportunity to grow as competent and productive learners as they engage in a cultural practice that matters to them?" It provided African American adolescent girls with the opportunity to develop social and academic competencies as they unwittingly met several learning standards. The chapter looks at the rewards of out-of-school time programs that provide youth with opportunities "to carve out free space" (Richardson, 2003) and engage and perform in meaningful and culturally appropriate activities.

THEORETICAL FRAMEWORK

Why is hair so important to African American women and girls? According to Banks (2000), scholars relate the importance of hair to its complex connections to "Africa, construction of race, enslavement, skin color, self esteem, ritual, esthetics, appropriate grooming practices, images of beauty, politics, identity, and the intersection of race and gender" (Banks, 2000, p. 7). African American hair practices are significant because they provide ways to contest "mainstream notions of beauty" (Banks, 2000, p. 28). For example, in the 1980s, Black women in corporate America adopted cornrows and braids to signify their African cultural heritage (Byrd & Tharps, 2001).

Other African American women associate doing hair with cherished rituals (Byrd & Tharps, 2001; hooks, 2001; Rooks, 1996). Author and social activist bell hooks (2001) writes that hair pressing, a process for straightening hair, is an important ritual in African American women's culture. Contrary to the notion that it is a denial of African American natural hair, hooks describes hair straightening as a process of building community, "an exclusive moment when Black women (even those who did not know one another well) might meet at home or in the beauty parlor to talk with one another" (hooks, 2001, p. 111).

Educators have asserted that literacy activities should connect to young people's cultural lives (Delpit, 2002, Lee, 2004). Carol D. Lee argues for a greater implementation of literacy instruction for African American youth based on their cultural practices (Lee, 2004), although cultural practices within the African American community may differ based on class, age, and geographical region. Lee suggests that practitioners observe routine practices used by African American youth and find ways to creatively incorporate them into a learning environment. For example, she observed that some African American youth engage in "signifying," a verbal strategy that includes indirection, irony, and humor. Lee used these observations to develop a culturally responsive instructional model using signifying in literacy learning environments (Lee, 1993).

Jabari Mahiri (1998) observed that the discourse of many high school students was influenced by rap and hip hop culture. His research focused on "the positive aspects of rap music relative to its thematic content, its critical voice, and its oral and written styles and performances" (Mahiri, 1998, p. 112). With the assistance of two eleventh grade teachers, Mahiri had students complete a questionnaire whose analysis helped educators create a curriculum that both legitimated rapping as a cultural practice and motivated youth to engage in critical thinking, reading, and writing.

PROGRAM CONTEXT AND DESIGN

The afterschool reading and writing workshop took place at a community center located in a predominantly poor working-class neighborhood in inner city Nashville. According to the community center's 2004 report, 88 percent of the residents are African American, 7.5 percent white, 0.1 percent Native American/Pacific Islander, and 3.15 percent other. The percentage of student enrollment with out-of-school suspension rate was over 35 at the two local middle schools. According to the 2000 U.S. Census Bureau, the poverty rate within this community was almost three times higher than the overall poverty rate of the county and state.

The community center began in 1993 and provides educational programs, arts and crafts, games, and athletic programs for young people. The center has wellness programs, educational programs, and social activities for senior citizens. The community center also provides infant and toddler daycare for working parents, job training for adults and teenagers, and job opportunities for young people ages fourteen to twenty-one. The staff includes an executive director, youth directors, social workers, sports coaches, high school student employees, college students and community volunteers, and early childhood teachers and assistant teachers. The community center opens at 6:00 AM and closes at 8:00 PM. The young people who come to the center after school play sports in the gymnasium, work on the computers in the computer room, receive reading instruction in the reading room, or homework assistance in the resource room.

In keeping with the center's educational goals, the executive director gave me approval to facilitate an afterschool reading and writing workshop in the conference room. Two months before the workshop, I attended a parent open house at the community center and two regular meetings with community leaders to get their support in recruiting adolescent girls. I also distributed colorful brochures describing the workshop and its benefits.

Ultimately, ten African American adolescent girls, ages twelve to sixteen, participated in the workshop sessions; five girls participated regularly. The one-hour sessions took place on Tuesdays and Thursdays in the community center's conference room. Most of the girls regularly attended afterschool programs at the community center before the project began. Most attended a public school close to the community center; eight were in middle school and two in high school. Over half said that they had scored below average in the reading component of the Tennessee Comprehensive Assessment Program achievement test and were therefore required to take a remedial literacy course for a minimum of two years. After each workshop session, the participants were served a light dinner.

Staff

I was the teacher-researcher in the afterschool reading and writing workshop. I am a certified K–6 teacher and was, at the time, a doctoral student in education. I have approximately two years of classroom experience in both the elementary and middle school grade level in the Philadelphia Public Schools. As a middle school substitute teacher, I taught sixth graders language arts and social studies. Before the workshop began, I established a relationship with the staff and directors at the community center. I volunteered at the community center in the summer of 2003 as a literacy facilitator and a reading tutor for a few of the children between ages nine and eleven. Most of the staff and youth knew me at the center and referred to me as Ms. Daneell.

Program Activities

In planning this reading and writing workshop, I selected a thematic topic that was meaningful and inviting to adolescent girls, as well as aligned with cultural interests. Building on the works of such educators as Alvermann, Young, Green, and Wisenbaker (1999), Delpit (2002), Lee (1993), and Mahiri (1998), I developed a literacy program designed to legitimize participants' cultural practices.

The workshop had four main objectives:

- To provide African American adolescent girls with the opportunity to talk, read, and write about a cultural topic that is typically not sanctioned in school;
- To promote critical thinking by inviting girls to view hair from cultural, historical, and sociopolitical perspectives;
- To encourage the girls to reflect on their reading and writing experiences about hair;
- To give the girls an opportunity to share their knowledge with others.

The reading and writing workshop included the components of a "focus unit" (Moss, 1995) modified to meet my four objectives. A focus unit "is a series of literary experiences organized around a central focus (a literary theme, genre, author, topic, or narrative element or device)"

(Moss, 1995, p. 53). In the original design of the reading and writing workshop, the focus unit consisted of four components:

A read-aloud experience

Self-selected reading experience

Journal writing

Creation of an original text

In early workshop sessions, the first thirty minutes were set aside for the instructor to read aloud followed by group discussion. Most of the passages I read to the girls came from *Tenderheaded: A Comb-Bending Collection of Hair Stories* (Harris & Johnson, 2001), a book of poems, stories, comics, and folktales about hair. The purpose of the read-aloud experience was to model fluent reading and to encourage the girls to relate the text to their lived experiences, to question the authors' stance, and to stretch their thinking.

After the read-aloud experience, which ran for approximately fifteen minutes, the girls began independent or buddy reading. They generally chose their own picture books, chapter books, or colorfully illustrated nonfiction books about hair care. They rarely selected nonfiction books that emphasized the historical, social, cultural, and political aspects of black hair because those books had "over ten chapters" and no illustrations.

For the journal-writing component, I gave each girl a decorated notebook in which she could respond to questions and ideas. This journal was to help her reflect on experiences in the workshop. The amount of time set aside for journal writing varied from session to session; the girls also had the opportunity to write during the first two components and during the last fifteen minutes of each session. Toward the end of each session, the girls typically volunteered to read their journal entries to the group.

The final component of the focus unit was designed to allow the girls to share their knowledge with others. The original text the girls chose to create was a television commercial held in a beauty shop, which would serve to inform others about what they had learned in their rich discussions about hair. The girls brainstormed and exchanged ideas, wrote their lines, and rehearsed in the last four workshop sessions. The girls presented their commercial on the last day of the workshop, named "Thank-You Day" by one of the girls to let me, as facilitator, know that they appreciated their three-month experience.

ACADEMIC STANDARDS

The afterschool workshop was clearly aligned with a number of academic curriculum standards. Because the workshop was held in Nashville, Tennessee, I have chosen to focus on the Tennessee State Board of Education Curriculum Standards for Grades 7–8.

Social Studies

Tennessee State Social Studies Standard 1.0 indicates that students will "understand the complex nature of culture." Culture is defined as the "similarities and differences among people including their beliefs, knowledge, change, values, and traditions." There were many activities in the workshop that were aligned with this standard. For example, a comparison between the function of hair in West African countries and in African American communities allowed the adolescents to gain a deeper understanding of the similarities and differences between the two cultures. We compared West African people's views of hair in the 1800s with the views mentioned in a popular songwriter's lyrics, India Arie's "I Am Not My Hair." After the workshop, a student, Shanika, enthusiastically surmised that she never knew that hair "was like a language" that West Africans used to communicate with each other.

The workshop is also aligned with the social studies standard requiring students to learn about the history in the United States during the nineteenth century. For example, in a workshop session about the life of enslaved Africans and hair, the participants were given a discussion sheet with questions that served as a comprehension guide as the girls read a chapter on "Hair in Bondage" (Banks, 2000). The girls were challenged to understand general information about the topic of slavery and then engage in critical discussions about this topic as it related to hair and skin. These questions were not only used to assess the participants' learning in the workshop session but also fostered social interaction as the girls asked me and each other questions about the topic.

Tennessee State Social Studies Standard 6.0, which aims at understanding how "personal development and identity are shaped by factors including culture, groups, and institutions," was embedded in several workshop activities. The participants were frequently encouraged to engage in discussions about the influence African American hairstyles had on corporate culture and vice versa. They discussed how African American women might be a part of the same cultural group, yet have a distinct identity. This was emphasized when the discussion covered understanding the statistic that 70 percent of African American women straighten their hair rather than keep it in its natural state. They discovered that "white envy" (Harris & Johnson, 2001) was not necessarily the primary reason for hair straightening, but that personal, social, and economic reasons influenced the decision each woman made about hair.

Language Arts

Tennessee State Language Arts Standard 1.0 states that students must be competent in "reading and listening skills [that are] necessary for word recognition, comprehension, interpretation, analysis, evaluation, and appreciation of print and nonprint text." Its focus is on language and listening skills, developing reading fluency, expression, and confidence, and developing and sustaining a motivation for reading. The reading component of the workshop in which participants select their own reading material and engage in sustained reading supports this standard. The participants frequently read in pairs or small groups during this time. Not only did these girls read to gain knowledge, but also they frequently shared their knowledge with others in the workshop. They were engaged in active learning, responding to texts by engaging in discussion and performing original skits, or reading other texts, which strengthened their reading comprehension.

Tennessee State Language Arts Standard 2.0 states that students will "produce written language that can be read, presented to, and interpreted by various audiences." In the workshop, each participant was given a reflective learning journal in which they wrote as they read books or listened to instructions. The participants chose to use the journal primarily to summarize the main ideas in texts, as a learning log. A few of their written reflections were presented orally to others in the workshop. On one occasion, a student wrote a poem that received such high accolades by the group that copies were made for each individual to take home. In the last few workshop sessions, I began engaging in written dialogue with each participant in their journals to support reading comprehension and critical thinking.

YOUTH DEVELOPMENT

The workshop exemplified many youth development principles. The workshop supported youth's social practices and cultural interests, provided them opportunities to hold empowering roles both collectively and individually, and encouraged learning with and from peers and the instructor. This informal learning environment provided many opportunities for personal and social development. Moreover, the hair workshop tapped into the participants' motivation, as well as provided them with an opportunity to make choices.

Social Competence

The reading and writing workshop on hair promoted social competence. The participants were encouraged not only to satisfy their personal interests but also to consider the interests of others through collaborative learning. Collaborative learning provided them opportunities to work as a team and learn negotiation skills. For example, the final project completed by the participants was primarily generated and refined by the group. Through collaborative efforts, participants brainstormed and developed the scenes they wanted to include in the commercial; as well, they made collective decisions about the props, characters, and script.

The workshop also promoted negotiation skills. Rather than constantly giving the girls directives regarding who should read or have access to materials and supplies in the workshop and for how long, I frequently encouraged the girls to work these issues out among themselves. In another example, I brought in a mannequin with real hair. The mannequin came with the name "Miss Jenny" written on its neck. After an intense negotiating session, the girls agreed to name the mannequin Tia Lafred. In the following session, they proudly expanded the name to Princessa Tia Lafred. I often observed them negotiating over who would style Princessa's hair and for how long.

Critical Thinking and Problem-Solving Skills

In the workshop session, I asked participants about real-life controversial issues and asked them to discuss how they would solve them. For example, I asked how they would respond if they were a parent and discovered that a classroom teacher of a different cultural background introduced to their child a book titled, *Nappy[1] Hair*. Not only were participants able to reflect upon and come up with multiple solutions for this and other problems, they discussed problems they personally faced in schools. The girls received, in most cases, a sympathetic ear as well as suggestions and recommendations on how to approach situations at school. Although some of these topics were around the issue of hair, the topics were often about more general racial and gender issues that were of concern to participants.

High Expectations

Although the girls' initial motivation for participating in the workshop was their interest in hair, this was only the starting point. One student mentioned that she attended the workshop to become "culturistic." When one of the girls asked her to clarify, she stated, "to get to know more about our culture." The reading materials were often high level—including readings by cultural critics and feminist authors. The ultimate aim was to raise the bar—to have participants think deeply about a cultural topic often presented as neutral.

I introduced highly sensitive topics, such as intraracial tensions about skin complexion and the notion of "bad" and "good" hair in the African American community. In a reunion with the girls, two years after the workshop, we delved into the topic of the role of slavery and hair. The purpose of the session was to challenge them to understand the magnitude of the brutal conditions of enslaved Africans in America through the topic of hair. Throughout the discussion, I reminded them that I was talking to mature young ladies about a serious issue and expected them to engage in

---

[1] A derogative term used to describe kinky hair.

a serious discussion. The girls lived up to the challenge and my high expectations.

Opportunities to Become a Leader

The girls were provided opportunities to take ownership of the workshop and of their learning. Atwell (1988) writes that learners need ownership, or control and power, over a space. The girls viewed the workshop as their own. They were free to talk, to create and modify rules, to offer suggestions on how to conduct the workshop, and to keep their peers in check. Fostering African American adolescent girls' sense of ownership and leadership may require allowing them to codesign workshops with an adult facilitator. For example, the girls began to do round-robin reading, which allowed them to assume control. Though some girls liked having adults read aloud so that the book could be finished quickly, when the text was something they liked, they wanted to savor it like a good meal in the company of friends.

OTHER BENEFITS AND COMPETENCIES

Opportunities to Explore Identities

The workshop gave participants the opportunity to explore who they were and who they might become. The participants were able to explore vocational, gender, and ethnic roles—explorations that might not be offered in a school setting. The exploration of identity was accomplished by establishing a democratic learning environment that invited a range of ways of expression, including the use of urban youth language or "hip hop language." In addition, the workshop helped girls assume identities that were not typically found in a traditional classroom setting. For example, in one session, the girls initiated a round-robin style reading, with each girl reading one chapter of *Junie B. Jones Is a Beauty Shop Guy* (Park, 1998). As they took turns reading, they turned the room into a beauty shop. Mia braided Princessa's hair, stopping only to read her self-assigned chapter aloud. Girls who were not reading from the book were styling each other's hair. As the two copies of the book circulated among the girls, so did the girls' roles in the workshop, as they served as readers, hairstylists, clients, fashion critics, talkers, and listeners.

Opportunities to Perform

As the workshop progressed, I observed that the participants were not engaged in my read-aloud activity. They essentially took over this process, and began to do round-robin reading, with each girl taking a turn reading aloud to the group. Round-robin reading has been cast unfavorably in literacy research (Opitz & Rasinski, 1998), but the girls had distinct reasons for favoring this format. All the girls, even those who said they hated to read, stated that they liked to read out loud. A number of them admitted that they like the way they sounded when they read and liked to have others listen to them. Rather than modeling fluent reading as classroom teachers do traditionally in read-aloud activities, the girls sought to take center stage (Goffman, 1959) and to perform for each other, even if they did not read fluently.

The girls chose to do literacy in many different ways than I had planned. They preferred to discuss first and then read, and then they preferred to read to each other rather than to listen to me or to read silently. I recognized that giving up some power as teacher allowed these literacy practices to bloom. It gave students the opportunity to perform literacy—to bring it to life—with their peers.

SUMMARY

Though over half of the girls in the workshop were relegated to a remedial literacy class in school, and few were truly interested in reading, five of them held sustained interest in the reading and writing workshop over a three-month period. One reason for this interest, I believe, is that the reading and writing workshop validated the girls' interest. The workshop was also successful because of its highly experiential aspect. The hands-on activities were not only an extension of the literature but helped the participants to focus on the topic. Finally, I believe they were highly engaged in the activities because they felt accepted. Delpit (2002) argues that educators' negative responses to children's language often result in the children's "rejection of the school language and everything they [schools] have to offer" (Delpit, 2002, p. 47). The workshop's success suggests that school educators, community members, and out-of-school time providers would be well served by validating young people's culture and by acknowledging the interest of African American girls in these types of topics.

Educational settings can and should embrace adolescents' social and cultural practices. In doing so, educators will encourage youth to accept more willingly the social practices adults value, such as reading and writing. Drawing from social and cultural topics as the basis of out-of-school time activities affords participants a safe environment where they can learn with and from each other as well as the instructor. These types of activities allow youth to appropriate and modify school-like practices to meet their own needs and interests. My experience with this workshop suggests that afterschool programs can and should use adolescents' cultural practices and interests to engage young people in literacy practices while allowing participants to choose the kinds of practices that best meet their needs.

Replication in Other Contexts

The afterschool reading and writing workshop can easily be replicated for upper elementary, middle school, and high school youth. If the workshop takes place in a community center, church, library, or school, the afterschool practitioner may consider implementing the following eight steps:

1. Develop clear objectives for the workshop. Review and consider how to use academic learning standards and youth development principles.

2. Determine how often the participants will meet. Will you meet daily, weekly, or biweekly (twice a week) with participants? Consider the duration of each session. Determine how many sessions you would like to have.

3. Gather resource materials. These include
   • Books on hair, skin, and beauty. (With older adolescents, you might consider selecting novels by Toni Morrison that provide an entry point to begin discussions about hair, skin, and beauty.)
   • Writing materials (i.e., journal books, pens, markers)
   • Artifacts such as a mannequin doll
   • Hair supplies for doll
   • Multimedia technologies (including CDs and DVDs that focus on the topic of hair, skin, and beauty)

4. Select a small group of youth (including males) who are interested in the topic.

5. Set at least two sessions before the workshop to receive recommendations from prospective participants and communicate your expectations for the workshop.

6. Follow the focus unit (see Moss, 1995) as a framework with adaptation. (See the earlier discussion.)

7. Consider the issue of space. Carefully determine how physical space and materials within the space will be arranged to make a comfortable and welcoming learning environment.

8. Meet regularly with participants about the workshop to discuss their and your expectations, and be willing to make adjustments. Please keep in mind that the selected participants, whether African American, Latina(o), or from another ethnic or social group, may hold different expectations of a hair workshop. For example, through collaborative discussions you may discover that the participants may be less interested in becoming "culturistic" and more interested in approaching the topic of hair and beauty from other perspectives, such as a feminist perspective, an historical perspective, or a scientific perspective.

References

Alvermann, D., Young, J. P., Green, C., & Wisenbaker, J. M. (1999). Adolescents' perceptions and negotiations of literacy practices in after-school read and talk clubs. *American Educational Research Journal, 36*(2), 221–264.

Atwell, N. (1988). *In the middle: New understanding about writing, reading, and learning* (2nd ed.). Portsmouth, NH: Heinemann.

Banks I. (2000). *Hair matters: Beauty, power and Black women's consciousness.* New York: New York University Press.

Byrd, A., & Tharps, L. (2001). *Hair story: Untangling the roots of Black hair in America.* New York: St. Martin's Press.

Delpit, L. (2002). No kinda sense. In. L. Delpit & J. K. Dowdy (Eds.), *The skin we speak* (pp. 29–48). New York: New York Press.

Ferrell, P. (1999). *Kids talk hair: An instruction book for grown-ups and kids.* Washington: Cornrows & Co.

Goffman, E. (1959). *The presentation of self in everyday life.* New York: Doubleday Anchor Books.

Harris, J., & Johnson, P. (Eds.). (2001). *Tenderheaded: A comb-bending collection of hair stories.* New York: Pocket Books.

hooks, b. (1999). *Happy to be nappy.* New York: Hyperion Books.

hooks, b. (2001). Straightening our hair. In J. Harris & P. Johnson (Eds.), *Tenderheaded: A comb-bending collection of hair stories* (pp. 11–115). New York: Pocket Books.

Lee, C. D. (1993). *Signifying as a scaffold for literary interpretation: The pedagogical implications of an African American discourse genre.* Urbana, IL: National Council of Teachers of English.

Lee, C. D. (2004). African American Students and Literacy. In D. Alvermann & D. Strickland (Eds.) *Bridging the gap: Improving literacy learning for pre-adolescent and adolescent learners grades 4–12* (pp. 70–85). New York: Teachers College Press.

Mahiri, J. (1998). *Shooting for excellence: African American and youth culture in new century schools.* New York: Teachers College Press.

Moss, J. F. (1995). Preparing focus units with literature: Crafty foxes and author's craft. In N. L. Roser & M. G. Martinez (Eds.), *Book talk and beyond* (pp. 53–65). Newark, DE: International Reading Association.

Opitz, M. F., & Rasinski, T. (1998). *Goodbye round robin: 25 effective oral reading strategies.* Portsmouth, NH: Heinemann.

Park, B. (1998). *Junie B. Jones is a beauty shop guy.* New York: Random House.

Richardson, E. (2003). *African American literacies.* New York: Routledge.

Rooks, N. (1996). *Hair raising: Beauty, culture, and African American women.* Newark, NJ: Rutgers University Press.

RESOURCES

Recommended Books on Hair

Picture or Literature Books

Dejoie, P. (1997). *My hair is beautiful, because it's mine.* Berkeley, CA: Group West.

Deveaux, A. (1987). *An enchanted hair tale.* New York: HarperTrophy.

Grimes, N. (1997). *Wild, wild hair.* New York: Scholastic.

Herron, C. (1997). *Nappy hair.* New York: Dragonfly Books.

hooks, b. (1999). *Happy to be nappy.* New York: Hyperion Books.

Tarpley, N. A. (1998). *I love my hair.* Boston: Little, Brown.

Yarbrough, C. (1979). *Cornrows.* New York: Putnam & Grosset.

Books on Hair Care and Maintenance

Bonner, L. B. (1990). *Good hair: For colored girls who've considered weaves when the chemicals became too ruff.* Oakland, CA: Sapphire Publications.

Collison, M. N.-K. (2002). *It's all good hair: The guide to styling and grooming Black children's hair.* New York: HarperCollins.

Ferrell, P. (1996). *Let's talk hair: Every Black woman's personal consultation for healthy growing hair.* Washington, DC: Cornrows & Co.

Ferrell, P. (1999). *Kids talk hair: An instruction book for grown-ups & kids.* Washington, DC: Cornrows & Co.

Fletcher, B. (2000). *Why are Black women losing their hair?* Seat Pleasant, MD: Unity Publishers.

Lee, B. (1988). Straight and nappy: Good and bad hair. On *School Daze* [CD]. Hollywood, CA: EMI Manhattan Records. (Lyrics printed in S. Lee & L. Jones (Eds.), *Uplift the race: Construction of* School Daze, New York: Fireside)

Morrow, W. L. (1973). *400 Years without a comb: The untold story.* San Diego, CA: California Curl.

Young Adult Nonfiction

Arnoldi, M. J., & Kreamer, C. M. (1995). *Crowning achievements: African arts of dressing the head.* Los Angeles, CA: Fowler Museum of Cultural History, University of California, Los Angeles.

Banks, I. (1999). *Hair matters: Beauty, power, and Black women's consciousness.* New York: New York Press.

Bryd, A. (2001). *Hair story: Untangling the roots of Black hair in America.* New York: St. Martin's Press.

Jacobs-Huey, L. (2006). *From the kitchen to the parlor: Language and becoming in African American women's hair care.* New York: Oxford University Press.

Jones, L. (2003). *Nappyism: Affirmations for nappy headed people and wannabes!* Dallas, TX: Manelock Communications.

Rooks, N. (1996). *Hair raising: Beauty, culture, and African American women.* Newark, NJ: Rutgers University Press.

Resources on Constructing a Literacy Program

Lee, C. D. (1993). *Signifying as a scaffold for literary interpretation: The pedagogical implications of an African American discourse genre.* Urbana, IL: National Council of Teachers of English.

Lee, C. D. (2000). African American students and literacy. In D. S. Strickland & D. E. Alvermann (Eds.). *Bridging the literacy achievement gap, grades 4–12* (pp. 70–85). New York: Teachers College Press.

Mahiri, J. (1998). *Shooting for excellence: African American and youth culture in new century schools.* Urbana, IL: National Council for Teachers of English.

Moss, J. F. (1994). *Using literature in the middle grades: A thematic approach.* Norwood: MA: Christopher-Gordon Publishers.

Moss, J. F. (1995). Preparing focus units with literature: Crafty foxes and author's craft. In N. L. Roser & M. G. Martinez (Eds.), *Book talk and beyond* (pp. 53–65). Newark, DE: International Reading Association.

Moss, J. F. (2002). *Literary discussions in the elementary school.* Urbana, IL: National Council for Teachers of English.

Roser, N., & Martinez, M. (Eds.). (1995). *Book talk and beyond: Children and teachers respond to literature.* Newark, DE: International Reading Association.

Strickland, D., & Alvermann, D. E. (2004). *Bridging the literacy achievement gap grades 4–12.* New York: Teachers College Press.

Tatum, A. (2005). *Teaching reading to Black adolescent males: Closing the achievement gap.* Portland, MA: Stenhouse Publishers.

6

Fabulous Fashions

Links to Learning and Life

Anne L. Thompson

"I feel famous," Margarita[1] exclaimed as she rushed to her family in her short, light blue dress, tiara, and high heels. "You look beautiful!" her mother said. Her father added, "You did a great job! We're proud of you." Margarita beamed.

Scenes like this were playing out all around the auditorium. Forty girls who participated in the Fabulous Fashions program at the Champions Academics Sports & Arts Club at a public middle school in New York City had just completed a 1970s-themed fashion show. The girls chose a theme, researched the era, traveled to a fashion museum, sketched designs, sewed their clothes, and staged a full-scale fashion show, complete with pounding music and the middle school version of a catwalk. The girls knew they had done something special. They knew Fabulous Fashions had taught them valuable lessons in how to design and create clothes. But they had little idea that their work in the fashion class had also enhanced a range of competencies that were aligned with academic learning standards.

This chapter will describe the Fabulous Fashions program and discuss how a youth development program during the out-of-school time can enhance traditional academics and address the roles of interest and

---

[1] Names of all program participants are pseudonyms.

self-esteem in enhancing student learning and engagement. That this program focuses on fashion is important not only because middle school girls are immersed in the topic but also because of fashion's potential to serve as a bridge for future careers. I was the site supervisor for the program for three years, and, impressed by the overwhelmingly positive response to the program, I wanted to take an in-depth look at how a single afterschool program such as Fabulous Fashions has the potential to significantly affect participants' lives.

THEORETICAL FRAMEWORK

Howard Gardner's (1983) theory of multiple intelligences helps explain why different activities work better for different children. Gardner posits the existence of seven types of intelligence: linguistic, logical/mathematical, spatial, bodily/kinesthetic, musical, interpersonal, and intrapersonal. All people possess all seven intelligences, but in different degrees (Gardner, 1983). By engaging many of Gardner's intelligences, the Fabulous Fashions program provides entry for participants with widely diverging aptitudes.

Participants with strong logical/mathematical intelligence, for example, who search for patterns and are more comfortable when things are quantified, flourish on the measurements needed in fashion design. Those with keen spatial intelligence do well too, as at all stages of a design project, from sketching through completion, participants have to visualize how the resulting product will look.

Researchers suggest that the incorporation of sensorimotor experiences, in which participants' senses and motor skills are engaged in an activity, increases attention, interest, and emotion (Wilson & Wilson Horsch, 2002). Participants with strong bodily/kinesthetic intelligence, who need to touch things to learn about them and would rather practice a skill than read about it, thrive in this type of program. The fact that they have to be out of their seats, manipulating fabric, and sewing to execute their designs provides excitement and motivation. Students' bodies, as well as their minds, are fully integrated into their work. As Reema, one of the participants said, "In fashion the teacher shows something to you; in school they don't show you, they tell you. It's better in the afterschool program because you can imagine or visualize it, and you have this thing in your hand to measure."

Participants who learn best through social and interpersonal learning are also encouraged in the Fabulous Fashions program. The learning environment and group structure promotes collective work. In addition, the fashion show, the major end product, has to be produced collaboratively. Yet participants who learn best intrapersonally can also work alone on their own designs at their own pace. Finally, Fabulous Fashions calls on participants to bring together all of their multiple intelligences to look at problems in a variety of ways.

PROGRAM CONTEXT AND DESIGN

The middle school where the afterschool program takes place is located in Castle Hill in the northeast section of the Bronx, New York. Castle Hill is a diverse community that is largely Hispanic and African American, but it has significant Asian and white populations as well. Per capita income is low, as are the numbers of high school and college graduates. Many residents are recent immigrants and speak a language other than English at home.

In many ways, the middle school reflects the makeup of the community, 50 percent of participants are Hispanic, 34 percent African American, 14 percent Asian, and 2 percent white, according to the *2002–2003 Annual School Report*. Many participants are English language learners. It is a Title I school, and, within the New York City schools, it has been classified as a high-need school. Eighty-one percent of its students are eligible for free lunch, and attendance rates are lower than the city average. At the time of this writing, the school was at 113 percent capacity (although it subsequently dropped to 91 percent). At that time, the average suspension rate for city schools was 43 per 1,000 participants; at this middle school the rate is 180 per 1,000. Crimes requiring police involvement were more than double the city average. Seventy-three percent of fifth through seventh graders failed to meet state English language arts standards, as did 77 percent of eighth graders. Participants enrolled in Fabulous Fashions were typical of students at the school. Some were enrolled in the college preparation program, but many were poor and failing one or more subjects or having disciplinary problems.

In 1998, the Sports & Arts in Schools Foundation, a nonprofit organization that provides afterschool and summer programs at New York City public schools, instituted the Champions Academics Sports & Arts Club. This comprehensive afterschool program runs for three hours every school day, serving 300 participants. Most of the funding was provided by The After-School Corporation, and some came directly from the Sports & Arts Foundation. Staff includes teachers and paraprofessionals from the school, as well as adults and college participants from the community, sports specialists, and parent volunteers. The program maintains a 12:1 student-to-instructor ratio. The program has maintained a strong relationship with the school through several changes of principal. School administrators have been supportive of the program's goals and have shared space, supplies, and expertise with the program.

Each day, after a group snack, fifth and sixth graders spend their first period engaged in sports and arts activities ranging from judo to "car art" to tennis, while the seventh and eighth graders participate in homework help and academic enrichment. Homework help groups are led by college honors participants and supervised by a teacher from the school. At 4:30, the participants "flip": fifth and sixth graders move to homework help while seventh and eighth graders proceed to sports and arts.

Each activity group meets two or three times a week. Participants choose their sports and arts activities, though they are generally required to remain in the activity they choose for a full season, which lasts approximately three months. With three such seasons each year, participants can explore activities in depth, while still experiencing a variety. In the Champions Club, sports and arts are seen as more than recreational; they are skill-building activities through which participants can acquire and hone new skills, consider whether these skills are something they might want to build upon in high school, and develop life-long passions.

In 2000, fashion design was added to the sports and arts offerings. Looking specifically for ways to engage girls, the site director spoke with program participants about their likes and dislikes, and nearly all the girls raved about fashion. Fashion design is offered three times a week; participants who enroll are required to attend all three sessions. Age groups are managed by having younger participants attend first and then go to homework help as the older participants come into the fashion program. As a fashion show nears, participants might all work together for the entire three-hour block of time. Participants may participate in as many seasons of fashion design as they choose.

Staff

Fabulous Fashions has been led by the same instructor since its inception. Mrs. Field is a professional fashion designer, not a school teacher. She generally works with one adult assistant, who is usually a parent or community member, and several participants recruited from nearby colleges, who serve as role models as well as instructors. While volunteers are encouraged, they are not a regular part of Fabulous Fashions. Mrs. Field's relationship with her participants is of particular importance to the success of Fabulous Fashions. Program participants adore her, although she is not warm or motherly toward them. She treats them as professionals and discusses little but fashion with them. She sets very high standards and expects all participants to meet them. She helps participants when they need it but expects them to take charge of their work and produce their own outfits for the show.

Underneath her professional demeanor, Mrs. Field is a fierce advocate for Fabulous Fashions. She constantly lobbies the afterschool program site director, the Sports & Arts Foundation, and funders for more money, more fabric, and more sewing machines. On her own time and often unpaid, she takes participants on trips around the city to museums or fashion exhibitions. She helps girls who are interested in obtaining a place in specialized public high schools to prepare their portfolios, and she calls schools on their behalf.

Program Activities

Mrs. Field's program model changed since its first inception. In the early days of the program, she spent a great deal of time on sewing, as opposed to true fashion design, using simple projects such as pincushions and hand-sewn fabric roses to teach basic skills. However, she realized that participants were most interested in clothes, so now they do one introductory sewing project, practicing the rudiments of sewing on simple skirts or tube tops, and move quickly to more advanced clothing designs. She also spent a great deal of time early on teaching participants how to work the program's six sewing machines safely. Now that she always has a base of participants who know how to use sewing machines, she simply offers a brief overview of machine safety and lets older participants mentor newer ones.

Early each season, Mrs. Field meets with participants from all four grades to decide on a theme for their fashion show at the end of the season. Past themes include the 1960s, the 1970s, Hawaiian wear, patriotism, formal wear, and hip hop. Mrs. Field reserves veto power; every year she turns down requests for a swimwear show. Once the theme is selected, participants gather information about fashions related to the theme. They use the Internet to find articles and scour fashion magazines for pictures. Topics such as the 1970s are also a great opportunity for parents to share their experience. For example, one student based her white swingy dress design on a picture of her father in a white outfit like the one John Travolta wore in the film *Saturday Night Fever*. Mrs. Field also brings in readings, pictures from her personal collection, and her own designs. Research and reading continue throughout the season as participants refine their ideas.

Once participants have some design ideas, Mrs. Field gives each student a *croque,* a sketch of the body. Participants draw their designs onto the figure, and she gives them feedback. She helps participants compose a detailed picture of a fashion design they want to create, determining the proportions, colors, and style. Mrs. Field then brings in fabric she has been acquiring. With her help, participants examine the fabric choices and decide which are the most appropriate for their designs. Mrs. Field helps participants make or use patterns and measure and cut their fabric, which is then sewn by hand or on a machine. Depending on their designs, participants might be making buttonholes, sewing zippers, casing elastic, or performing other complex tasks.

The atmosphere is both social and intensely serious. Participants work in small groups at their own pace, talking a bit to their friends. Participants chat as they sew, but they sew or design the whole time. Some are hunched over sewing machines, some are hand stitching or basting, others are sketching designs or looking through magazines for inspiration. Although they have the opportunity to goof off, few do. In fact, participants I spoke with said they did not like one student because she was often talking and fooling around, rather than working on her sewing. Student work is almost completely self-directed, in contrast to their teacher-directed work during the school day.

As they create their outfits, participants are also planning their fashion show. They choose the music and create the backdrop. Mrs. Field discusses how to model to best show off clothes, and participants practice. They then choreograph the entire elaborate production. All participants who complete their outfits are in the show, which provides a strong incentive to finish their work. The rare student who does not want to be in the show can work backstage or hand out programs. Finally, participants present the show to an audience of family, friends, classmates, the principal, and the PTA.

All enjoy participating in Fabulous Fashions and are extremely proud of their work. When I asked participants whether they liked the activity and why, their responses included "It is fun", "It makes me feel happy", "I feel different, like nobody else", and "I feel like I have a special talent." Participants said they enjoyed the class; they agreed that they were proud of themselves for what they had accomplished. Fabulous Fashions has a high rate of reenrollment, and many participate for more than three seasons. As Monique, one of the participants said, "I can't wait to get school over with so I can get to fashion."

Fabulous Fashions has a written curriculum designed to enhance academic skills. It consists of fifteen lessons that address such topics as the history of fashion in the twentieth century, street fashion as observed in the *New York Times,* how fashion changes show the evolution of women's roles, types of fashion shows, elements of design, marketing and merchandising, and fashion careers. Since the Champions Club tries not to overwhelm participants with academics, the teacher and homework tutors implement this curriculum selectively, based on the academic backgrounds and interests of Fabulous Fashions' participants, as well as on their schedules and time constraints.

ACADEMIC STANDARDS

Fabulous Fashions ties directly into many academic learning standards. Although these standards vary from state to state, there is a great deal of overlap. Fabulous Fashions takes place in the Bronx, New York, and thus the New York State Standards are most applicable.

Language Arts

New York State Language Arts Standard No. 1 provides that "participants will read, write, listen, and speak for information and understanding." It provides that "participants will collect data, facts, and ideas; discover relationships, concepts, and generalizations; and use knowledge generated from oral, written, and electronically produced texts."

As they research their fashion show outfits, participants are acquiring knowledge aligned with this standard. For example, one activity requires participants to research five artistic career options: fashion designer, jewelry designer, make-up artist, graphic artist and architect. Participants do research using books, trade magazines, and the Internet, and they also interview professionals in the clothing industry. They produce written reports about careers and create a product. In another example, a student may be required to write copy and produce the promotional posters. Thus Fabulous Fashions provides participants with a content area that is highly interesting, yet it engages participants in acquiring skills outlined in the standards. Finally, fashion has its own vocabulary, such as the word "*croque*." To build this vocabulary, Mrs. Field displays a "word wall" where participants define and post new terms and vocabulary.

Social Studies

Fabulous Fashions activities are also aligned with the social studies standards. New York State Social Studies Standard No. 1, for example, provides that "participants will use a variety of intellectual skills to demonstrate their understanding of major ideas, eras, themes, developments, and turning points in the history of the United States and New York." Many Fabulous Fashions activities support this standard, but one is particularly on point. In the unit "Evolution of Fashion," participants are divided into groups and read several articles about a decade in history and its fashions. They also review pictures of the fashions. Participants then complete a chart, noting three historical events and three fashion trends from the era. For example, the entry for the 1960s might read like this:

Events	*Fashion Trends*
Civil Rights Movement	Tie Dye
Flower Power	Twiggy Look
Travel to the Moon	Long, straight hair

Participants then make fashion cards, drawing two images, one of an historical event and the other of a fashion trend. During their unstructured program time, they play card games such as *Go Fish*, trying to accumulate all the cards of a particular decade. As they play with the cards, they are exposed to images from the entire past century. And, as already seen in the 1970s- and 1980s-themed fashions shows, students can create designs based on the knowledge they gain about each decade.

The Arts

Engaging youth in art, in particular, seems to be a powerful way to support a range of social and academic competencies. There is some indication that the arts can help participants from low-income communities achieve academically (Catterall, Chapleau, & Iwanaga, 1998; Catterall & Waldorf, 1999; Heath, 1998;). While New York State Arts Standards do not address fashion design specifically, Fabulous Fashions supports the general arts learning standards. For example, New York State Arts Standard No. 1 encompasses this key idea:

> Participants will make works of art that explore different kinds of subject matter, topics, themes, and metaphors. Participants will understand and use sensory elements, organizational principles, and expressive images to communicate their own ideas in works of art. Participants will use a variety of art materials, processes, mediums, and techniques, and use appropriate technologies for creating and exhibiting visual art works.

Participants in the fashion design class must master such visual elements as color theory, perspective, proportion, and design; the result is a personal, creative expression in fabric rather than on paper or canvas. In addition, fashion shows can display elements of both dance and drama. Fabulous Fashions calls on participants to explore different topics of their choice through multiple sensory venues—fabric, design, and clothing construction. Participants then have to convey their thoughts through a finished product, reflecting, for example, the youth culture of the 1960s or the values of traditional African communities. Thus participants are complementing the standards-driven arts projects of their school day with the chance to explore related topics through a range of media.

YOUTH DEVELOPMENT

Fabulous Fashions embodies many youth development principles. It springs from the interests of youth, capitalizes on their strengths rather than on deficits, and sets standards that are achievable through scaffolded experiences with expert guidance. The afterschool program, a space between home and school, is a community institution that plays a key preventative role, particularly with urban youth in distressed communities, such as the one at the middle school described in this chapter. In this context, youth can develop caring and supportive relationships with adults in a range of roles, not just that of teacher. In addition, participants, through their engagement in youth development activities, have the opportunity to contribute and participate in their neighborhoods and communities.

Activities at afterschool programs can foster internal competencies known to support resiliency and positive youth development. For example, working as a team on the fashion show enhances social competency. The strong vocational aspect of the project can foster a sense of purpose and future, helping youth envision a life in which they learn a trade, a skill, or go on in their schooling. Rather than feel powerless as they struggle to achieve a remote standard that does not necessarily relate to their daily lives, participants set and work toward goals they personally value.

Creative and Cognitive Benefits

Perhaps most clearly, Fabulous Fashions provides youth with the opportunity to develop their creative interests. Participants must call upon their artistic talents to produce quality end products. But beyond the creativity required by fashion design, Fabulous Fashions provides cognitive benefits. Participants have the opportunity to think about topics in a variety of ways and from multiple viewpoints rather than linearly to reach a single outcome. In addition, participants can call upon their individual and group talents to articulate and achieve their visions. For example, after participants decide upon a fashion show theme, they then control the research process and determine the end product.

Opportunities to Succeed

Fabulous Fashions provides youth with multiple avenues to success. First and foremost, it gives them a showcase in which to display their products, a place where their work is valued and evaluated by an audience. Participants who may not be successful during the school day are provided an opportunity to excel and shine. Participants can select a simple design or a complex outfit, depending upon their skill levels, which allows those having different skill levels an equal chance for success. Further, the fact that participants control the whole fashion show, from choreography to décor, allows them alternate pathways to express their personal competencies and exercise leadership. Participants can decide where they want to focus their efforts and access the support they need as they work toward their own goals.

Youth Culture

Fabulous Fashions' multiple-year popularity and high retention rate demonstrate that it is truly aligned with youth culture and interests, and the program itself shows participants that what they value is important. The applause the participants hear at the fashion show validates the hard work that went into producing their outfits, and it also validates their youthful interest in fashion. The fact that adults they respect are, in turn, showing respect for participants' interests and abilities improves student self-esteem and makes them more likely to work harder in other areas.

Clear, High, and Realistic Expectations

As a requirement, participants are expected to produce an outfit that is appropriate to wear in a show before parents, teachers, and others. Further, if they do not finish their outfit, they simply do not participate in the show. Expectations are clearly articulated up front, and failure to meet those expectations has direct ramifications. Participants I spoke with did not feel intimidated by these standards; rather, because adults expected them to achieve and they believed the adults had realistic expectations, they determined that they, indeed, had the ability to produce high-quality work.

Choice and Decision Making

Participants make individual decisions about whether to join Fabulous Fashions. Allowing participants to make such a choice signals that they are capable of making good decisions for themselves and that adults trust and respect their opinions. Also, participants have a great deal of say in determining the theme of the fashion show and the attire that will be worn. The notion of choice is firmly aligned with the youth development principle of autonomy, that is, the "ability to act independently and exert some control over one's environment" (Bernard, 1991). While participants receive constructive guidance, in the end, they shape the direction and presentation of the fashion show. Once they see the show is a success (historically all have been), they realize that they are indeed capable of making decisions and that their work is appreciated by the larger community.

OTHER BENEFITS AND COMPETENCIES

Self-Esteem

Mastering moderately difficult tasks and creating high-quality products lead to feelings of competence and pride (Graham & Weiner, 1996). Some participants in the program had grown accustomed to failure; many who showed me their report cards were happy that they had failed only one subject. In contrast, participants felt successful in Fabulous Fashions. Anyone who attends the fashion show can see that participants feel good about themselves, as illustrated in the vignette that opens this chapter.

Participants were proud of the way the clothing they made demonstrated their mastery of fashion design. To determine the quality of their work, participants compared it with their mental images, decided whether it looked and hung correctly, determined whether the stitching was correct, and so on. What they did not do was to compare their clothes to those made by other participants. This mastery standard for success, as opposed to one where participants judge their worth by comparing themselves to others, is linked to positive student achievement (Stipek, 1996).

Despite the importance of skill mastery, peer recognition also furthers confidence and pride. Many participants of Fabulous Fashions talked about peer reaction to their fashion show. Participants said they sometimes felt like celebrities in school the day after a show. While parents and teachers may have appreciated how hard participants worked, their peers were the ones who most appreciated the finished product—the clothes.

Student pride was reinforced by family reaction. At the fashion show, parents cheered from the minute the first student took the stage to the finale. Afterward, families rushed backstage to praise the participants. After the 1970s show, I heard comments such as, "I'm proud of you," "Nice work," and "You looked like a professional designer." Participants said these comments made them feel "proud and pleased," "even more confident," "happy I did this work for something," "like a professional," and "confident, pretty, and that I should not give up." Since middle school is a difficult time for children, particularly girls, this positive family reaction is especially critical.

Envisioning Careers

The "realness" or authenticity of fashion to participants is key to the popularity and impact of Fabulous Fashions. Fashion design is real in that participants can wear the clothes they make; its practical, hands-on training can lead to a specific career or, at least, create a pattern of thinking about the future. John Dewey, the progressive educator, was an early proponent of integrating vocational work with traditional academics (Dewey, 1915). Dewey believed that school was too divorced from the reality of participants' lives but that purely technical training was too limited in a world where jobs rapidly become obsolete. He argued that the skills participants need in order to thrive in the world are adaptability, ingenuity, and creativity, and that such skills are most likely to arise from a combination of hands-on and theoretical approaches.

Most participants in Fabulous Fashions are thinking about future schools and careers. All but one of the twenty-seven participants had thought about high school, even though the fifth and sixth graders were years away from the prospect. Of these, seven were interested in fashion high schools and six in arts-related high schools. Participants also thought beyond high school. Having visited the Fashion Institute of Technology, many hoped to attend. They were also interested in other specialized colleges such as Parsons School of Design, Mrs. Field's alma mater.

In discussing their career plans, participants said they planned to be fashion designers and some wished to be models. Participants also said they intended to pursue other arts such as dancing, acting, and singing. One student planned to open her own fashion design shop. In fact, she had planned her career down to the details, as she wrote in a paper for one of her school-day classes:

> If I had a business, I would have a fashion company. It would be named Fashions by Kathy. I really don't think I will hire more than 14 people to work at my company. Some of the people I hire will be family members because some also want to be fashion designers. My business will be in a very big space where everybody can see it. I would want to be famous because of what I do and because of my store.

Of course, the careers young people eventually pursue are not necessarily the ones they consider in middle school. The important point is that Fabulous Fashions enables participants to begin to create strategies for and to visualize their future. One of the most important results of Fabulous Fashions may be the fact that 93 percent of participants polled—participants who live in a high-crime area and attend a high-needs school, participants whose parents have generally not attended college and have unfulfilling jobs—felt hopeful about the future. By making academic and career options a part of everyday conversation and by being grounded in a framework of positive youth development, Fabulous Fashions allows participants a vision of a successful, productive future.

Connections to the Community

Fabulous Fashions creates a natural bridge to participants' communities and families. All participants said that they talk about Fabulous Fashions with those at home, creating dialogue at a time when the lines of communication may be beginning to fray. Over half of the participants had sewed prior to enrolling in the program, and most were taught by family members, including mothers, grandmothers, and, in two cases, fathers. In some neighborhoods, such as Chinatown, parents often work for long hours in the sweatshops and clothing factories. The Fabulous Fashions program can allow them to share their expertise with their children. In addition, clothes are often a key to national origin, and this project provides an opportunity for both parents' work and ethnic heritage to be recognized and validated by their children.

In a striking example of clothes linking two generations and two countries, Helana's mother, born in Bangladesh, wore traditional clothing in her home country. Here in America, she gave the garments to her daughter to make into Americanized clothing for a fashion show.

SUMMARY

Fabulous Fashions takes a topic that adults might consider "fluff" and transforms it into an educational tool. The program fosters critical thinking and social skills, motivation, self-esteem, and planning for the future in participants whom traditional methods have often failed to reach. By placing learning in a context that participants can see, touch, and enjoy, Fabulous Fashions can provide them with greater enthusiasm and capacity for achievement both after and during school.

In our increasingly standards-based world, afterschool programs such as Fabulous Fashions remain havens where young people can develop their own interests and strengths, and at the same time hone academic and social competencies. The trick is to base programs in youth development principles and endow such afterschool experiences with meaning: to go beyond the catwalk to use student curiosity, interest, and motivation to cultivate intellectual and social growth in all of its incarnations. If we equip participants with tools to use in a context they enjoy and enable them to feel confident about their abilities, we will both foster their success in traditional academics and allow them to explore their world in person-ally meaningful ways.

Replication in Other Contexts

Replicating an afterschool activity in a new location can often be a challenge. In gen-eral, activities that are too reliant on a charismatic instructor or need extremely site-specific materials or resources that are difficult to re-create. Replicating a fashion program, in particular, may seem daunting to many, especially to those who do not live near a major fashion center such as New York City. But, in truth, Fabulous Fashions can work in a wide variety of settings. Of course, local adaptations are important to ensure that the program will fit the needs and talents of any particular community.

In replicating Fabulous Fashions, we must consider three key components: the instructor, supplies, and space. Hiring a qualified fashion instructor may seem a partic-ularly challenging task. There are, however, two different and effective approaches to find-ing instructors. First, programs can hire someone who already has a great deal of sewing or fashion design experience. Family members—mothers, fathers, grandmothers—often have excellent sewing skills and would be thrilled to share them with an eager young audience. Often family members are available on a part-time basis and eager to work in the location where their child or grandchild goes to school. Hiring a family member as a program instructor also improves links between program and commu-nity and generates income, which goes right back into the community.

There are other ways to locate qualified instructors; for example, you can post a job advertisement in local fabric stores. Employees at fabric stores are often aware of people in the community who know how to sew and are interested in part-time work. Many community colleges and adult education programs offer sewing and design classes; both professors and college students may be interested in work-ing in an afterschool program. The Home Sewing Organization at www.sewing.org offers a searchable database of sewing educators that have completed the organi-zation's Trained Sewing Educator program. You can also contact a local chapter of the American Sewing Guild at www.asg.org.

If you cannot find a qualified instructor, you can help develop one. Programs can train current staff members to provide basic sewing or design classes. Many fabric stores and adult education or parks and recreation programs offer inexpensive introductory classes. The Internet offers a great deal of information about sewing classes in regions throughout the country. Although hiring a sewing novice certainly has drawbacks, as long as projects are kept simple, they can often be executed by individuals with limited sewing experience.

In addition to an instructor, supplies are an important, and often expensive, necessity in a fashion design program. The following items are critical to a basic class: fabric, straight pins, scissors, needles, thread, tape measure, seam ripper, and

(Continued)

(Continued)

patterns. Also important, but not essential, are sewing machines, bobbins, an iron and ironing board, a dress form, zippers, buttons, a cutting board and rotary cutter, a hem marker, and a seam gauge.

It is not always easy for programs to obtain necessary supplies at a reasonable price. One option is to ask participants, parents, and teachers at your program to bring in any excess fabric or other materials they have at home. Other than that, your best option is to shop the sales, whether in actual stores or on the Internet. Joann's has stores throughout the country, and also has a Web site, www.Joann.com, that offers discounts. Also, eBay® offers a tremendous variety of fabrics and basic sewing tools at generally reasonable prices.

The other fashion program essential is space. Participants need large, clear, flat workspaces, solid chairs, appropriate lighting, and a storage area for projects that are not yet complete. At the middle school described in this article, participants used the cafeteria, which was, in many ways, ideal: the tables were large and moveable and had attached benches. The lighting was strong and direct. Because of its good relationship with the school, the program was able to secure storage space, although Mrs. Field did store many materials in her car. The key to good storage is negotiating for it up front and keeping materials organized to maximize its use.

Here are some more specific tips to keep in mind if you are trying to replicate Fabulous Fashions:

1. You do not need as many sewing machines as you might think—or any for that matter. Participants from the middle school described above preferred hand sewing, and sewing machines were often idle.

2. Do not expect silence as participants work; sewing is an inherently social activity, as evidenced by the historical popularity of quilting bees.

3. Display samples of projects before participants begin, so they can have a concrete goal in mind.

4. Teach participants basic safety before they begin class; this is especially important when using sewing machines.

5. Display completed samples of student work to reward participants and inspire others. It is ideal if you can display work by ALL of the children in your program.

6. A culminating event is critical—even if you do not put on a fashion show, it is important for children to display their hard work to an appreciative audience.

7. Fashion has its own vocabulary; if possible, display a word wall where participants can define and post new terms

When replicating Fabulous Fashions, remember that the most important part of the project is student engagement. The needs and interests of your participants will direct your program. And once your program has run for a few years, you may discover that you have created a whole group of engaged and experienced instructors right in your own community.

References

Bernard, B. (1991). *Fostering resiliency in kids: Protective factors in the family, school and community*. San Francisco, CA: Far West Laboratory for Educational Research and Development & the Western Regional Center for Drug-Free Schools and Communities.

Catterall, J. S., Chapleau, R., & Iwanaga, J. (1998). Involvement in the arts and human development: Extending an analysis of general associations and introducing the special cases of intensive involvement in music and the theatre arts. In E. B. Fiske (Ed.), *Champions of change: The impact of the arts on learning* (pp. 1–18). Washington, DC: Arts Education Partnership and the President's Committee on the Arts and Humanities.

Catterall, J. S., & Waldorf, L. (1999). The Chicago Arts Partnership in Education (CAPE): summary evaluation. In E. B. Fiske (Ed.), *Champions of change: The impact of the arts on learning* (pp. 47–62). Washington, DC: Arts Education Partnership and the President's Committee on the Arts and Humanities.

Dewey, J. (1915). *The school and society.* New York: Dover Publications.

Gardner, H. (1983). *Frames of mind: The theory of multiple intelligences.* New York: Basic Books.

Graham, S., & Weiner, B. (1996). Theories and principles of motivation. In D. C. Berliner & R. C. Calfee (Eds.), *Handbook of educational psychology* (pp. 63–84). New York: Simon & Schuster Macmillan.

Heath, S. B. (1998). Living the arts through language and learning: A report on community-based youth organizations. *Americans for the Arts Monographs, 2*(7), 1–18.

Stipek, D. (1996). Motivation and instruction. In D. C. Berliner & R. C. Calfee (Eds.), *Handbook of educational psychology* (pp. 85–113). New York: Simon & Schuster Macmillan.

Wilson, L. M., & Wilson Horch, H. (2002). Implications of brain research for teaching young adolescents. *Middle School Journal, 34*(1), 57–61.

RESOURCES

There are a number of organizations that can serve as resources to sewing and fashion programs.

> American Sewing Guild
> 9660 Hillcroft, Suite 510
> Houston, Texas 77096
> (713) 729–3000 (phone)
> (713) 721–9230 (fax)
> www.asg.org

The American Sewing Guild (ASG) is dedicated to the belief that sewing is a rewarding and creative activity. The ASG has chapters around the country, and its Web site is a good source of links to a variety of other resources.

Crochet Guild of America
1100-H Brandywine Boulevard
Zanesville, Ohio 43701–7303
(740) 452–4541 (phone)
www.crochet.org

The Crochet Guild of America is dedicated to preserving and advancing the art of crochet. It has local chapters around the county and provides correspondence courses for members. You can also order patterns through the Web site.

Home Sewing Association
P.O. Box 1312
Monroeville, Pennsylvania 15146
(412) 372–5950 (phone)
(412) 372–5953 (fax)
www.sewing.org

The Home Sewing Association is committed to getting people sewing by providing inspiration and education. The Web site offers sewing projects, tips on learning how to sew, and a valuable database through which you can search for local educators.

Sew America!
P.O. Box 943
Monroeville, Pennsylvania 15146
(412) 372–5950 (phone)
(412) 372–5953 (fax)
www.sewamerica.org

A newly formed organization, Sew America! sponsors activities that involve sewing in strengthening communities. Its goals are to promote interest in and awareness of sewing, to develop and engage in fundraising projects in furtherance of its mission, and to develop and fund programs and materials related to practitioners of the sewing arts. Sew America! intends to work with afterschool programs and serve as a grant-making organization.

For more information about the middle school program Fabulous Fashions and its curriculum, please contact

Sports & Arts in Schools Foundation
58–12 Queens Boulevard
Woodside, New York 11377
(718) 786–7110 (phone)
(718) 786–7635
www.sasfny.org

Index

**CORWIN
PRESS**

The Corwin Press logo—a raven striding across an open book—represents the union of courage and learning. Corwin Press is committed to improving education for all learners by publishing books and other professional development resources for those serving the field of PreK–12 education. By providing practical, hands-on materials, Corwin Press continues to carry out the promise of its motto: **"Helping Educators Do Their Work Better."**